The Battles for Empire
Volume 2

The Battles for Empire
Volume 2

Battles of the British Army through the

Victorian Age, 1857–1904

ILLUSTRATED

Robert Blackwood

and

James Grant

LEONAUR

The Battles for Empire
Volume 2
Battles of the British Army through the Victorian Age, 1857-1904
by Robert Blackwood and James Grant

ILLUSTRATED

FIRST EDITION

Leonaur is an imprint of Oakpast Ltd
Copyright in this form © 2023 Oakpast Ltd

ISBN: 978-1-916535-04-6 (hardcover)
ISBN: 978-1-916535-05-3 (softcover)

http://www.leonaur.com

Publisher's Notes

Contents

CHAPTER 1

The Relief of Lucknow: 1857

Quickly the Indian revolt spread from garrison to garrison, and the native mind was inflamed with hatred of the British. At Lucknow the native troops waited a considerable time before taking any definite step, but trusting to the success which had attended the mutineers at Delhi, they at last took the fatal plunge. On 31st July, 1857, large numbers of the 13th, 48th, and 71st Infantry regiments left the cantonments without orders, along with two troops of the 7th light cavalry. They fled in hot haste to Seetapore, but were hotly engaged by a party of Europeans under Brigadier Handscomb, who was killed in the encounter.

All sorts of stories were now in circulation to inflame the native mind. According to the chiefs and *fakirs*, a vast army was marching on India to enforce the greased cartridges and compel the natives to become Christians. That as the Crimean war had made a great many widows in Britain, the queen intended to marry them to the chiefs of Oude, so that their children might be brought up Christians and inherit the land. To a Briton these tales seem ridiculous, but it must be remembered that the Native Indian mind is easily turned when caste and religion is concerned.

It was a trying time for the British officers, for well they knew that their men might revolt at any moment. One officer sums up the situation in the following words:—

In the battlefield men stand alone to face the danger, but there are our wives and families involved in the same risk with ourselves, requiring our protection and our care, and necessarily withdrawing our thoughts from the actual work before us, while their helpless state fills us with the deepest anxiety.

Lucknow at the time of the mutiny was regarded as one of the most

7

important cities. The gilt domes of the mosques and the mausoleum of Asoph-ud-Dowlah gave it a gay appearance when viewed from a distance, but the situation is bad, the soil being white sand, which is driven about by the wind, often completely enveloping the city. It is situated on the south bank of the Goomtee River, where it is navigable at all seasons of the year. A great force of rebels now commenced to gather before the city, and proceeded to invest the Residency.

Sir Henry Lawrence, who was in command, was prepared for the attack, and had placed the buildings formerly occupied by the Resident and his suite in a complete state of defence. A large stock of provisions had been laid in, and the walls were as well fortified and mounted with guns as they could be, A number of the native troops had remained "true to their salt," and they apparently took as much interest in the preparations for defence as their white comrades. The rebels made many determined attacks, and kept up a steady fire, which fortunately did little damage. When they came to close quarters, they suffered severely, Sir Henry inflicting a number of heavy defeats upon them.

Day by day the siege dragged on, the enemy, strongly reinforced, becoming bolder, despite their losses. Sir Henry had a large number of helpless women and children in his keeping, and at last the provisions, which they trusted would last until relief came, began to run out. Something had to be done, and the brave Lawrence resolved that at all events the women and children should not starve while he had men to fight for them. A sortie upon the rebel camp was agreed upon, so Sir Henry, at the head of only 200 men of the 32nd Cornish Light Infantry, and supported by the loyal native infantry and a few guns, sallied forth to the attack.

The affair was short and sharp, but to the point, The advance guard of the rebels was engaged, and, unable to stand the fierce onslaught of the Cornish bayonets, they fled in total rout, leaving many dead and wounded upon the field. A great quantity of livestock was captured, and, well pleased with the success of his foray, Sir Henry prepared to return.

Just as the troops were re-entering the city, they were thunderstruck to have a murderous fire of grape shot poured in upon their ranks. What had happened? What was wrong? The questions were soon answered. For the fire proceeded from the guns which were in the hands of the native artillery, formerly supposed to be loyal. With the treachery which is so characteristic in the Oriental, the gunners turned the muzzles of their guns upon the returning band, and discharged volley after volley into the ranks, the fire being particularly directed against the 32nd. It was all over in a few minutes, the treacherous rebels who had posed as loyal soldiers of the queen, fleeing to augment the ranks of the mutineers.

They had done their cowardly work well, for upwards of sixty rank and file were killed and wounded, together with a dozen officers. Sir Henry Lawrence was wounded on the leg, and, unfortunately for the garrison, the wound proved mortal. Hopes were at first entertained for his recovery, but lockjaw set in, and this brave and dauntless officer died three days after receiving his wound.

The Europeans now realised that they had only their own good arms to trust to, so they determined to avenge the treachery, and defend the women and the children to the last. The lines commanding the town were abandoned, and the Muchee Bhaun fort, which had been strengthened, became the headquarters of the Lucknow defenders. There were 350 women and children to protect from the murderous rebels, and still there was no appearance of relief, yet the gallant 32nd, or all that was left of them, stuck to their posts.

Meanwhile how fares it with the relieving force under Havelock? This general, when he had sufficiently rested his troops at Cawnpore, resumed operations against Nana Sahib, whose palace and stronghold at Bithoor he destroyed by fire after capturing 16 guns, several elephants, and a few camels. He had but a slender force, and by sickness and wounds it was daily growing more feeble. Still, he gallantly pushed on in the direction of Lucknow, and reached Oonas, a little town whose only approach was guarded by fifteen rebel guns. Lucknow lay before, and there must be no turning back. The little force sprang at the guns with the bayonet, drove the enemy back in an irresistible charge, and the town was in Havelock's hands.

Resting but a few hours, he hurriedly pushed on to Busserut Gunge, where he found fresh opposition. The gateway was barricaded, and the road, which had been carefully trenched by the mutineers, was guarded by four guns. A stubborn resistance was made to his onslaughts, but the fire from the British guns terrorised the rebels, who, at the next charge, broke and fled, leaving Havelock master of the situation.

Yet dearly was the victory bought, for out of his small force he had eighty-eight officers and men killed or wounded. Sunstroke was playing havoc amongst the men, but the courage of the Highlanders was amazing under all conditions.

General Havelock's attack on Nana Sahib at Futtypore

An officer of the 78th (the Ross-shire Buffs) writing home, says:—

I can see the Highlanders are too much thought of here, for we get the brunt of everything. If there is anything to be done, the old general calls out, 'Highlanders to the front! Charge that battery! You only require the word from me. Soldiers, up and at them!' The word is no sooner said than done, for in the next moment the bagpipes are heard skirling, and our wild 'Hurrah!' resounding from the mountains; and look a little to the front and you will see the Scots charging up to the cannon's mouth. But many of these brave men never come back. Poor fellows! We have laid a great many of them in the dust since we came here; and peace be with them...The 78th did for the rebels, and sent them spinning in the air and on the road in all directions, and in three hours there was nothing of them to be seen but legs, arms, and heads.

With his enfeebled force, it would have been madness on Havelock's part to have gone further forward into the rebel-infested territory, so, on 5th August, he sorrowfully commenced his return journey to Cawnpore. Toiling on, they reached the Ganges, where they were again attacked by the rebels, who opened a terrible fire upon the 78th. The Highlanders did not stand idle as targets for the mutineers, but with a yell of rage and hatred they dashed at the guns, and once again the rebels tasted the terrible bayonet.

"Well done, my own brave Highlanders!" cried Havelock. "You have this day saved yourselves and your comrades."

The shattered force was allowed to proceed to Cawnpore without further molestation, and the expedition had not been in vain, for the rebel army which was besieging the Residency at Lucknow was drawn off to meet Havelock, thus allowing the garrison freedom to lay in provisions and strengthen the fortifications.

Havelock did not put off much time in resting, for, four days after his arrival, he set out a second time, at the head of 1,300 troops. Once again, the enemy were met at Bithoor, which Havelock described as "one of the strangest positions in India." The plain in front of the enemy's position was covered with thick sugarcane, which reached high above the heads of the men, while their batteries were defended by thick ramparts, flanked by entrenched quadrangles. The British, guns made little impression, but once again the bayonet made them flee, and the British pursued them for some distance, killing many in the wild rush.

The force returned to Cawnpore next morning, and took up a position on the plain of Subada, where Havelock issued a flattering note to the force to the effect that it "would be acknowledged to have been the prop and stay of British India in the time of her severest trial."

The force had nothing to do now but wait for reinforcements, and the soldiers chafed at the delay, especially as cholera broke out in the camp. The 78th, which had lost a large number of men, was strengthened by the addition of five companies from Allahabad, and were also supplied with Enfield rifles.

The 5th and 90th regiments arrived at Cawnpore in the beginning of September, while Sir James Outram, the "Bayard of India," also arrived to take command of the Cawnpore and Dinapore divisions. At once preparations were made for the third march on Lucknow, where the garrison was pluckily holding the rebels at bay. A bridge of boats was thrown over the Ganges, and on 16th September, Sir James Outram issued a division order in which he resigned to Havelock the honour of leading on the force to the relief of Lucknow, "in gratitude for and admiration of the brilliant deeds of arms achieved by General Havelock and his gallant troops."

Sir James accompanied the force as a volunteer, and the army of relief was divided into two brigades of infantry and one of artillery as follows:—1st Brigade of Infantry under Brigadier-General Neill—5th Fusiliers, 84th Regiment, 1st Madras Fusiliers and 100 men of the 64th Regiment. 2nd Brigade of Infantry, under Colonel Walter Hamilton of the 78th, consisted of the 78th Highlanders, 90th (Perthshire) Light Infantry, and the Sikh regiment of Ferozepore. There were three battalions of artillery, the volunteer cavalry, a few irregulars, and a small body of engineers.

At Lucknow, meanwhile, the Presidency had been converted into a fortress, but the never-ceasing fire of the rebels told severely upon it. The walls were perfectly riddled with shot, and a number of the women and children who had taken refuge there were killed. The master mind of Sir Henry Lawrence was sadly missed, and with the heavy fire and a spreading pestilence, the lot of the defenders was most desperate. There was need of relief, so, leaving the imprisoned garrison, we will follow the fortunes of Havelock. Leaving Cawnpore in the keeping of the 64th regiment, the force crossed the Ganges, and were exposed to a galling fire from the enemy who, however, retreated to Mungulwar.

The real advance commenced on the morning of the 21st September, and the rebels were soon discovered in their old position at Mungulwar, which they had strongly fortified. The position, however, was soon carried, the rebels offering but slight resistance. The cavalry pursued the fleeing mutineers, and cut down scores, while four guns and a colour were captured, the British loss being very slight. Through a monsoon of rain which lasted for three days, the force pushed on over the scenes of their former struggles, passing Buseerutgunge and the village of Bunnee.

On the afternoon of the 23rd the enemy were descried in a strong position in the neighbourhood of Lucknow, at a place known as the Alum Bagh. It consisted of a large brick mansion, a mosque, a well, and a beautiful garden. Havelock's troops were now in sight of the glittering domes of Lucknow, and with light heart they prepared to give battle to the rebels in their path. The head of the column at first suffered from the fire of the enemy's guns, as it was compelled to pass along the trunk road between morasses.

The force quickly deployed into line, and our guns coming up, a heavy fire drove the enemy back. The 2nd Brigade advanced through a sheet of water, and drove back the enemy's right, while the 1st Brigade successfully attacked the front. Five guns were taken, and ultimately the enemy retired towards Lucknow, pursued by Sir James Outram at the head of the cavalry. The British force was rested prior to an attack upon the city, but the force was subjected to a constant cannonading from the enemy's guns, which did so much damage that Havelock had to retire his left wing out of range. The sick and wounded, along with the camp-followers and baggage, were left at the Alum Bagh, guarded by a strong detachment of Europeans and Sikhs.

Joyfully did the poor unfortunates in the Residency hail the looming of Havelock's guns, and they redoubled their efforts to defeat the rushes of the rebels, who were now rendered desperate.

On the morning of the 25th of September, Havelock advanced on Lucknow, and found that the enemy had taken up a very strong position at the village of Char Bagh. It should be mentioned that the city of Lucknow is surrounded by a canal, and had the enemy broken the bridges, Havelock's task would have been more difficult, but as it was, they left them intact, contenting themselves by posting heavy guns to defend the Char Bagh bridge. The rebels were in great force, and occupied gardens and walled enclosures, from which they poured an incessant and destructive musketry fire upon our advancing troops.

Relief of Lucknow

The 1st Brigade led the attack under Neill, supported by Captain Maude's battery prepared for the attack, and dauntlessly rushed the bridge. Every obstacle was surmounted by Outram and Neill with their gallant fusiliers. The palisade was stormed, the gunners bayoneted, and the guns taken. Havelock followed up his advantage by bringing up the 78th and 90th, who rushed in impetuously to complete the work. Fighting every inch of the way, and subjected to a heavy musketry fire from walls and gardens, the Highlanders advanced, and after spiking the guns, hurled them into the canal. The houses on both sides of the street were occupied, the rebels slain by the bayonet, and their remains cast in heaps on the roadside.

From this point to the Residency was about two miles by the direct road, which lay through the city. Havelock knew that he had yet to encounter stern, resistance, and very soon found out that the crafty mutineers had trenched parts of the road, barricaded others, while every house was loopholed. One of their batteries had a deep pit immediately in front covered with bamboo, and sprinkled with earth, in the hope that the Highlanders, in charging the guns, would fall into the trap and become an easy prey.

Havelock, however, to avoid any danger, took another route, which lay along a narrow road on the left bank of the canal. The 78th was left to guard the bridge until the entire force, with ammunition, stores, etc., had passed.

The united column pushed on, detouring to the right, but did not meet with much serious opposition until the Kaiser Bagh, or king's palace, was reached. Here two guns and a strong body of the enemy opened fire with grape shot and musketry. Our artillery with the column had to pass a bridge exposed to this fire, but fortunately they were protected by the buildings adjacent to the palace of the Furrah Buksh. The fire from the battery was terrible, and our men were falling by scores. To make matters worse, a section lost their way through someone calling out, "Cavalry to the front!" Every house was a fortress, so the magnitude of Havelock's task may be imagined. Our men were desperate at seeing so many comrades fall, and many times they charged up to the walls and fired into the loopholes.

A party stormed and kept possession of the palaces of Furrah Buksh and Lehree Kothee, both of which proved useful. The night was now coming on, and the red gleams of fire lit up the scene.

In the meantime, the 78th found themselves hotly assailed. As soon as the enemy saw the movement of the main body, and perceived that only a small body was left at the bridge of the Char Bagh, they returned in large numbers to annoy the Highlanders. The 78th threw out two companies to occupy the more advanced buildings of the village; four companies were sent out as skirmishers, and the remainder held in reserve in the buildings near the bridge. It was hard work to get the carts and cattle over the narrow rough road. The enemy brought two guns to bear upon the regiment at 500 yards' range, and the advanced companies were soon engaged in a tornado of shot and shell.

There was nothing for it but to capture the guns, so the two advanced companies under Captains Hay and Hastings, pluckily charged up the street and at the point of the bayonet captured the first gun, while the skirmishing party coming to their assistance, silenced the remaining gun, which was spiked, the other being hurled into the canal. The 78th now retired to the bridge, with the wounded, leaving many dead upon the field. The entire line of carts having now passed, the 78th evacuated the bridge, and formed the rearguard of the force. This gave the rebels the opportunity of crossing the bridge, and, protected by a wall on the right bank, they enfiladed the road along which the force had to pass. They were now almost surrounded, but, under a galling fire, they pushed on, yet losing severely.

Havelock by this time had heard of the plight of his favourite regiment, and ordered the volunteer cavalry and a company of the 90th to their assistance. The lane, however, was too narrow for the operations of the cavalry, and they, too, began to lose men. At length a point was reached where four roads met, but as the British had no guides the officers had to trust to luck, and chose a road to the left, which appeared to be the most direct route to the Residency. They pushed on through a street composed of fine houses, which were loopholed and garrisoned, until they reached the Kaiser Bagh, where they came in reverse upon the battery which was firing upon the main body. After spiking the guns, the force crept under the walls of the Kaiser Bagh, being exposed to a belching fire from the palace, and was at last successful in rejoining the main body.

After a short rest Havelock decided that they must make an attempt to reach the Residency that same night. The 78th and the Sikhs were ordered to advance, and, led by Havelock and Outram, along with Neill and his fusiliers, they charged with desperate gallantry through streets of flat-roofed loopholed houses, from which a perpetual fire was kept up.

Another battery was captured, and every obstacle surmounted.

16

With a ringing cheer the relieving force entered the Residency, being joyfully welcomed by the garrison. Relief had come just in time, for the enemy had driven two mines under the chief works, and if these had been loaded and sprung, it would have been all over with the defenders.

Our loss was very severe, as upwards of 400 had fallen, including the gallant Brigadier Neill, who fell in the final charge on the Residency.

It was not until the next day that the remainder of the troops, sick and wounded, guns and baggage, could be brought into a place of safety. The enemy kept up a heavy fire, and rendered the march difficult and dangerous. After many desperate deeds, all were safe in the Residency, and the rebels, smarting under the treatment they had received, withdrew to positions on the outskirts of the city. The British flag had been kept flying, and the women and children saved from the bloodthirsty ruffians who anticipated a second Cawnpore.

Lucknow had been certainly relieved, but Havelock could not march back to Cawnpore, through a rebel-infested country, with such a large number of women and children, his sick and wounded, and with only a small force to guard them. There was nothing to do but wait at Lucknow for help in his mission. The troops were not idle, as the enemy were particularly daring at times. They were driven from the rear of the position, and the palace, extending along the line of the river from the Residency, was cleared and taken possession of, making excellent barracks for the troops.

On another occasion three columns of Sir Henry's force gave the enemy a surprise by attacking their works at three different points, destroying the guns, and blowing up the houses which afforded the rebels protection. The garrison had to be maintained on reduced rations, but there was not much fear of the defenders starving. The enemy had still one battery which remained in position close to the Residency, which annoyed the garrison by its fire. Its capture therefore became imperative, and a force of over 500 men under Colonel Napier of the Bengal Engineers, set out to capture it.

The column formed on the road leading to the Pyne Bagh, and, advancing to some houses near the jail, drove the enemy away from them and from a barricade under a sharp musketry fire. The column, having to work its way through strongly-barricaded houses, it was late before a point was reached from which the battery could be commanded. This position having been obtained, and it being discovered that the battery was in a high position, scarped and quite inaccessible without ladders, it was decided to postpone the assault.

The position which had been won, having been secured and loop-holed, the troops occupied the buildings for the night, and were subjected to a heavy fire from the battery, which somewhat disturbed the slumbers of the men.

They were fresh enough next morning, however, and prepared to advance upon the battery, covered by a heavy artillery fire from the Residency. A severe fire was opened from a barricade which flanked the battery on the right, but this being turned, the troops advanced and drove the enemy from the battery, capturing the guns, which had been withdrawn to some distance, and, driving off the enemy, who defended them to the last with musketry and grape. The guns having been destroyed and the house blown up, the force retired to their resting-place of the previous night.

Everything was now done by the garrison to strengthen it position. Barricades were erected at all available points, the defences of the Residency were improved, and every building put into a state of defence.

One of the greatest dangers the British had to guard against was the enemy's mines, which threatened the position from every possible quarter. The garrison had always to be on the alert, and were constantly employed in counter-mining. In this they were very successful, and managed to thwart the rebels at almost every point.

In regard to the mining operations, Sir James Outram, who was now in chief command, wrote:—

I am aware of no parallel to our series of mines in modern war; 21 shafts, aggregating 200 feet in depth, and 3,291 feet of gallery, have been erected. The enemy advanced 20 mines against the palace and outpost.

The 78th regiment, as it always did, played a prominent part in the defence, and were posted in a range of houses which were constantly under the heavy rebel musketry fire. The walls of the houses were riddled, but the Highlanders never flinched, and kept thousands of the fierce mutineers at bay. Day by day the siege dragged on, and scarcely a day passed but there was some assault or sortie. The rebels were being strongly reinforced by flying squads of mutineers from all parts, who were content to serve where they were safest in point of numbers. As yet they had made no impression on the garrison, but their numbers were becoming so numerous that Outram and Havelock became extremely anxious.

It is always when the cloud is at its blackest that the silver lining appears, and a message, whether it was false or true, reached the Residency that relief was near at hand. The soldiers cheered, and vowed to keep the flag flying.

LUCKNOW

Chapter 2

The Relief of Lucknow: (continued) 1857

Cooped up in the beleaguered city of Lucknow, the brave Havelock received but scanty news of what was transpiring in other parts of India. He certainly felt assured that the British Government would never leave him in that hopeless position, so he settled down to make the best of his situation and keep the rebels in check. It was a trying time for Outram and Havelock, for almost daily the death-roll was increased through wounds or disease.

Meanwhile Brigadier Greathed had been marching through the country, inflicting severe punishment on the mutineers who had fled from Delhi, where the British had won a great victory. The Mhow and Indore rebels were crushed at Agra, and the column which latterly moved from Mynpooree under command of Sir James Hope Grant, arrived at Cawnpore to hear of the precarious position of the British garrison at Lucknow. After one or two minor engagements, in which he inflicted some loss upon the rebels, Sir James determined to proceed to Lucknow, and attempt with his small force to relieve the city.

On 8th November, 1857, he arrived at the famous Alum Bagh, where Havelock had left his sick and wounded under the protection of the 64th regiment. Between this strong position and Lucknow there lay a large undulating plain, intersected by the canal which encircles the city. Yet that plain could not be traversed, for it was given over to the camping ground of a huge company of rebels. The mutinous force before Lucknow must have numbered almost 50,000, so that the task of relief was rendered impossible to the small British force.

It seemed galling that relief could not be given, with the Residency such a short distance away, but it would only have been courting annihilation to attempt to pierce the serried rebel ranks. Therefore, Hope Grant took up his position at the Alum Bagh to wait for reinforcements, and to be at hand should Havelock require aid. The two British forces were vastly outnumbered by the enemy, and it has never been satisfactorily explained why the rebels did not attack the Alum Bagh. The position was certainly a strong one, but the mutineers could with ease have invested it from all quarters, and at the same time maintained their pressure upon Lucknow. Possibly they had grown tired of fruitless besieging, and, confident in their numerical superiority, preferred to lie passively on the plain and wait for the attack.

Hope Grant knew that he would not have long to wait, for before leaving Cawnpore he was informed that the dashing and fiery Sir Colin Campbell was on the warpath, and was hastening as fast as he possibly could to form a junction with the troops in Oude, which now comprised Outram and Havelock's pent-up force in Lucknow and Sir Hope Grant's column at the Alum Bagh. Sir Colin, while travelling post haste to Cawnpore, ran a very narrow escape. He was impatient to get at the rebels, and, disregarding an escort, hurried on. He came across a detachment of the rebellious 32nd regiment, and was all but captured, having to take refuge in a post bungalow, where luckily, he found some of our soldiers, who were resting after a heavy march. Ultimately, he reached Cawnpore, and without further delay marched to Lucknow, where he now knew he should join Hope Grant. This desired junction was effected on 11th November, and Sir Colin immediately assumed command of the Lucknow relief force.

This relieving army was now considerably strengthened, and Sir Colin, trusting to active conjunction by Outram and Havelock from the Residency, determined to make the attack. His force consisted of the 9th Lancers, Captain Peel's naval brigade, Sikh cavalry, Hodson's Horse, 8th, 53rd, 75th, and 93rd regiments of infantry, two battalions of Punjaub foot, native sappers and miners, 10 guns of the horse artillery, 6 light field guns, and the heavy field battery of the Royal Artillery. Sir Colin left his baggage at the Alum Bagh in charge of the 75th, and was further reinforced by 700 men drawn from the Welsh Fusiliers and the 82nd Foot, two guns of the Madras artillery, along with a body of the Royal Artillery and Engineers.

The commander-in-chief advanced from the Alum Bagh in the direction of Dilkhoosha Park ("Heart's Delight"), a former hunting seat of the kings of Oude, with a castle situated on a beautiful eminence in the park. The advanced guard, which had been further strengthened by some companies of the 5th, 64th, and 78th Highlanders under Colonel Hamilton of the 78th, was soon brought into contact with the enemy, and, steadily advancing, was subjected to a heavy musketry fire from the rebels. The vanguard, however, cleared away this opposition, and drove the mutineers over the canal which runs through the park. The rebels fell back upon the Martinière College, but were unable to withstand the fire from our guns. This building was splendidly adapted for defence, standing secure and firm in the centre of a large thicket of mango trees.

The enemy seemed to be terrorised by the steadiness of our advance, and abandoned the college after a short conflict, in which they lost heavily. The mutineers seemed to have a wholesome dread of the Highlanders with their kilts and terrible bayonets. Many of them had never seen such men before, and were terrified by their appearance. They called them "petticoated devils," and many firmly believed that they were women sent over to avenge Cawnpore. At all events, the Highlanders were there, and they did much to strike terror into the hearts of the cowardly rebels.

The college having been so easily won, Sir Colin made the park his headquarters. Sir James Outram and Sir Henry Havelock were not idle inside the city, the force being busily employed in digging trenches and erecting batteries in a large garden held by the 90th regiment. These were concealed by a lofty wall, under which several mines were driven for the purpose of blowing it down when the moment for action should arise. It was determined by the generals that as soon as Sir Colin and his force should reach the Secunder Bagh, this wall should be blown down, and that the batteries should open fire upon the insurgent defences in front, when the troops would storm the Hera Khanah, the steam-engine house, and the king's stables.

Sir Colin had meanwhile arranged his force in the gardens to the best possible advantage as far as safeguarding against any attack, and being in readiness to make a dash for Lucknow at any time. On the 12th an attack was made upon his advance guard by a determined band of rebels. The field battery and Captain Peel's heavy guns came into action, and did great execution amongst the enemy. After the artillery had done its work, the 53rd and 93rd Highlanders, along with the 4th Sikhs, charged the enemy in daring style, causing them to break rank and fly. The 9th Lancers kept up the pursuit, and almost for the first time the rebels received a taste of the deadly lance. The rear guard now moved up, and a junction was formed nearer and ever nearer the city. At last Sir Colin determined to advance, and, as per arrangement his route was by way of the Secunder Bagh.

This is a strongly-fortified building, surrounded by a wall which was loopholed in every direction, fairly bristling with rifle muzzles. Brigadier Adrian Hope led the troops forward in skirmishing order, and this was the signal for a heavy fire from the enemy's guns. The British guns were quickly brought up by Captains Blunt and Travers, and replied vigorously to the enemy's fire. While this artillery duel was in progress, Hope made a dash at the head of his infantry, and drove the enemy from the boundary walls of the Seconder Bagh into the main fortified building.

It was here that the last stand was to be made, and the rebels knew that if they had to surrender there was no hope of mercy, for they were caught like rats in a trap. To the left of the Secunder Bagh the enemy held a line of barracks, which, in the possession of a trained force, might have offered great resistance.

The Sutherland Highlanders, supported by a company of the 53rd, rushed the building, and at the point of the bayonet drove the enemy helter-skelter from the position to the plain beyond, where the majority of them were killed. All had been success to Sir Colin's brave army up to now, and it was with a cheer that the men rushed to storm the Secunder Bagh, which was teeming with well-armed and desperate rebels.

Havelock had in the meantime exploded his mine, and through the breach his battery opened a withering fire upon the enemy's defences. Volley after volley was poured in, and this gave Sir Colin's troops the opportunity to make a great attack from his point of vantage. The 4th Sikhs, led by Lieutenant Paul, who fell while gallantly rushing forward, had the honour of opening the assault, while the 93rd and 53rd acted as supports. The Highlanders and Sikhs are staunch friends, and might be seen during this campaign going about camp arm-in-arm, the Sikh with the Scotchman's feather bonnet, and the Scot with his dusky comrade's turban. It is even related that they petitioned their captains to procure the Highland dress for them. It was but fitting then that the Sikhs and Highlanders should share the honours of this glorious attack.

Forward the Sikhs rushed, amid a hail of bullets, with the Highlanders close behind. The rebel fire was terrible, for they knew this was their last chance, and they could not expect mercy from our revengeful troops. A small breach had been made in the wall, but it was so narrow that only a handful of men could enter at a time. This did not deter our men, and the Highlanders, just a little bit jealous of the Sikhs that they should be the first to enter, ran a neck-and-neck race to the breach through the hail of bullets. They dashed up to the very loopholes, and from the gaining of this position the fate of the rebels may be said to have been sealed. The Sikhs, 93rd, 53rd, and the 90th Highlanders clustered round the doomed building.

The well-known author, Rees, gives a graphic account of the situation:—

Our men dashed in as quickly as the narrow breach permitted. They went under the very loopholes of the enemy, and, cunningly lying down while the enemy let fly a volley at the caps placed on their bayonets, and which our men put up as a target for the time being, they as soon as the enemy's fire was exhausted, and before they could load again, tore down the iron bars, broke up the barricades, and jumped down from the windows in the walls.

Then followed a terrible slaughter, for the rebels were so thoroughly cowed that they offered but little resistance. Here and there one more brave than his fellows would fire his rifle or attack with his *tulwar*. A bullet in his brain, or the terrible bayonet through his breast soon silenced him. The Highlanders were reeking in blood. Their faces were bespattered by drawing their gory hands over their perspiring foreheads as they momentarily paused in the conflict.

"This is awful!" exclaimed one soldier of the 93rd to his neighbour.

"G'wa, man! this is grand!" and he plunged his bayonet into a cringing wretch who begged for mercy. "Cawnpore, ye deevil!" he hissed, and turned to renew his work of slaughter.

It was the memory of Cawnpore that roused the Highlanders, and the Sikhs were every bit as bloodthirsty. The gateway, the large principal room, and a side room were deluged in blood, and littered with reeking corpses. The green tartan of the 93rd was of scarlet hue ere many hours had passed. The full extent of the silent slaughter with the bayonet may be judged when it is stated that nearly 3,000 bodies were dragged from the building on the following day. Cawnpore was avenged with interest.

The troops of the garrison had also been doing brave deeds. Fully 800 of the garrison had attacked other parts of the defences. Men like the 78th Highlanders were spoiling for a charge, and how they rushed upon their foes! The rebels reeled before the shock, and fled, leaving the buildings in our hands. Guns were mounted on the position thus gained, and on the following day opened fire on the observatory (Tara

Kottee) and the mess house. Captain Peel's naval siege train went to the front, and drew up within, a few yards of the loopholed wall of the Shall Nujuf, where a heavy and merciless fire was kept up upon the rebel defenders. After the mess house had been battered by our heavy guns, recourse was once more had to the bayonet, which was never known to fail. Nor did it on this occasion, for the position was soon gained and the enemy put to flight.

The task of relief was nearly completed, and madly our men rushed into the enclosure round the Motee Mahal (Pearl Palace), where the rebels made their last despairing stand. It was futile on their part to attempt to stem the rushes of the victorious British troops. They went down like grain before the sickle, and those who steered clear of the bayonet gave vent to yells of terror and fled to the plains, which were already dotted with bands of fugitives. The slaughter of the rebels had been enormous, but yet the killing of a few thousands did not diminish to any great extent the rebel horde which had ignominiously retreated to a place of shelter. The killed and wounded were but as a drop in the bucket, and although Lucknow was for the moment relieved, trouble was yet to be expected from the mutineers who clustered round the city.

Proudly Sir Colin met and grasped the hands of the fearless Outram and the gallant Havelock. With flashing eyes Havelock praised and thanked the relieving and defending troops. It was pointed out to him that his son was lying wounded, but the old warrior continued his address, although his heart must have been rent with anxiety about his son. Fortunately, it was only a slight wound, and the lad soon recovered, but the incident shows Havelock as the soldier, who thought it his duty to thank his soldiers before attending to his wounded son. Our great success had not been attended without loss, for we had 122 officers and men killed, and 345 wounded. Sir Colin's first care was for his wounded, and after consultation with Havelock and Outram, he decided to remove the toil-worn garrison to a place of safety. It was evident that it was not worth, while to hold the position against such a large investing army.

The tactics which he employed in carrying out a safe retreat show the wily old Sir Colin in his best colours. He was not afraid to meet the enemy again at the head of his brave troops, but, burdened with women, children, wounded and stores, he sought to avoid a conflict, and this is how he managed it.

On the 20th and 21st, he ordered Captain Peel's battery to open a heavy fire upon the Kaiser Bagh, and at the same time Havelock's battery in the palaces opened a tremendous fire upon the same position. Naturally the enemy expected an attack upon this point, and consequently concentrated there. The strategic old general bargained for this, and he silently withdrew the whole garrison. The retreat was managed without a hitch, and the force marched on with Sir Colin in the rear to direct any attack upon the force.

The enemy at last learned of the move, and tried to turn the rear at the Alum Bagh but failed. On arriving at that place, Sir Colin pushed on with his charges to Cawnpore, where he fought a decisive battle, which is described in the chapter dealing with Cawnpore. He left Sir James Outram behind with a strong force to check any movement on the part of the rebels.

The British camp was unexpectedly thrown into mourning through the death of Sir Henry Havelock. This brave and Christian general was worn out with the hardships and anxiety of the campaign and siege, and was stricken down with dysentery, to which he succumbed on the 24th November. Safe to say, there was no British officer so genuinely loved and respected by the rank and file. They adored him, and gladly would have died for him, and now that he was gone, they mourned him as only true friends can mourn.

Lucknow had now become the focus of the rebels, who were flying aimlessly about the country, avoiding actual conflict with British troops. Sir James Outram's division numbered almost 4,000 men of all arms, and he took up a strong position, being fortified at all points, the circuit of his entire position being nearly ten miles. Here the force remained for nearly three months, while Sir Colin, after retaking Cawnpore, was engaged recovering the Doab and making his final preparations for a final assault upon Lucknow.

These months were full of anxiety for Outram and his men, for they had to be continually on the alert against a mammoth army, which must have numbered close upon 100,000. Against less skilfully prepared fortifications they might have, by sheer force of numbers, overwhelmed the British, but, like whipped curs, they preferred to keep at a safe distance, and harry the British when opportunity came their way.

They made one feint bolder than their usual, which had for its object the surrounding of the force and the cutting off of supplies. Outram got to know of the scheme, and checkmated them at every point. Although vastly outnumbered, our force repelled every attack, and inflicted heavy loss upon the mutineers, besides capturing four guns and twelve ammunition waggons.

News came that Sir Colin was once again upon the march, and although the troops under Outram were confident that they could hold back the rebels for ever, they were glad at the prospect of being reinforced and led into the field by the great Sir Colin, He matured his plans carefully, and adopted a line of action which he thought would entail as little loss upon his army as was possible. With this end in view, he sent out strong detachments to all parts, with instructions to meet him at all costs at Lucknow on a certain date. Thus, Sir Hugh. Rose, General Hope Grant, and Colonel McCausland scoured the country and achieved several notable victories.

But perhaps the most glorious and decisive victory was gained by Brigadier Franks at the head of a force of 4,000 troops. He contrived to prevent a junction with two noted rebel leaders, Bund Hossein and Mhendee Hossein, by attacking the former at Chanda, in the Nagpore territory.

The enemy, consisting of 8,500 *sepoys* and a large number of mercenaries, occupied the fort and villages in front of the place. They were driven from this place, leaving behind 300 killed, along with six pieces of cannon. Franks prepared to encamp in this position, when he was surprised to hear the discharge of artillery, and a volley of grape shot crashed into his lines.

The other Hossein, unaware of his relative's defeat, had come up with 10,000 men and eight guns. Franks gave him battle, and in a very short time the rebel had to seek safety in flight. Later, he fought another battle with 25,000 *desperadoes*, including 5,000 trained *sepoys*, his force being 2,500 Europeans supported by 3,000 Nepaulese. He totally defeated them, and the enemy fled, leaving a *rajah* and 1,800 dead on, the field.

Twenty guns, the standing camp, baggage, ammunition, and all material of war were captured. It was almost a bloodless battle as far as Franks was concerned, for, incredible as it may appear, he only lost two men killed and three wounded.

Sir Colin marched from Cawnpore on the 28th February, 1858, at the head of almost 30,000 troops, including about 20,000 Europeans. He had 60 heavy guns and 40 field pieces, while his cavalry consisted of 1,500 Europeans and 3,000 native troopers. This imposing force was still further augmented by the infusion of 4,500 men under the redoubtable Franks, and fully 10,000 fierce and wiry Ghoorka warriors under the loyal Jung Bahadoor. The savage rebels knew that a big force was to be set against them, and they realised that every man. would die if he fell into the hands of the British. Rumours spread in their ranks that great red-haired men who were giants, with bare knees, were coming to kill them, and the chiefs had great difficulty in preventing them from fleeing.

Campbell appeared with the 2nd Division of infantry, cavalry, and a section of artillery at a position east of the Alum Bagh on 2nd March, and on the following day the attack on Lucknow commenced, the enemy abandoning Dilkhoosha, and falling back on the Martinière College. The Dilkhoosha was instantly occupied by the 42nd Highlanders (Black Watch), and a battery was soon at work from this position on the Secunder Bagh. Sir Colin, gratified at the arrival of Franks and the Ghoorkas, resolved to make attacks from the River Goomtee, which flows past the city. A pontoon bridge was thrown across, and 6,000 men and 30 pieces of cannon, under Sir James Outram, passed over. The enemy, as was expected, came out of the city in large numbers to check this force.

A heavy artillery fire and a dashing charge of the Queen's Bays sent the rebels back, and Outram was able to strengthen his position. It was an artillery duel during the next two days, the enemy's stronghold, the Martinière College, suffering severely from our shells. Outram had made good his position, however, for he advanced along the Fyzabad road, and, although meeting with stout and desperate resistance, he gained his end, which was the Badshah Bagh, or King's Great Garden, from which his guns had free play upon the whole line of entrenchments formed by the rebels at the canal, rendering them practically useless, besides turning the rebels' entire position.

Sir Colin now had up the naval brigade to deal with the buildings within the enclosure, from the windows of which the rebels kept up a harassing and deadly rifle fire. The mortars, howitzers, and battery guns had little effect, as the rebels, now fighting for dear life, remained wonderfully steady in the trenches.

"A taste of the steel, my men!" grimly exclaimed Sir Colin, as he turned to the Highlanders and Sikhs.

They steadied, and then, at the word, went forward in one silent, death-dealing line of steel. This was too much for the rebels, who fired a few random shots and fled, with the swift-footed Sikhs stabbing them as they ran. The Martinière was won by the bayonet, and with the chief rebel position there also feel the Residency, the Secunder

Bagh and Bank House. The Highlanders were once again conspicuous at the Secunder Bagh, which had withstood the thunders of the naval brigade guns. Two companies of Highlanders reached a platform, and were brought to a stop by the dead wall.

"Tear off the tiles! in at the roof, Highlanders!" cried Sir Colin.

This was enough for the brave fellows, and in a minute, they had vanished through the tiles and bamboo, and thus the Secunder Bagh was taken.

The enemy by this time were in almost total rout, and Hope Grant swept the surrounding country, cutting up the fleeing bands, while the artillery continued to blaze away at the buildings still infested by the desperate robbers and rebels. The Sutherland Highlanders, with dauntless courage, stormed the *begum's* palace, and swept aside the defenders with their trusty bayonets, which reeked with blood.

The gallant Outram held the Goomtee Bridge, and cut up the flying enemy unmercifully, while the Kaiser Bagh, which was almost an impregnable position in capable hands, fell easily, the rebels fleeing out of the city on the opposite side, only to be ruthlessly cut down by Sir Hope Grant's thousand sabres. The gallant little Ghoorkas won their spurs by the capture of the whole line of trenches which menaced the Alum Bagh, where our sick and wounded had been left.

An eye-witness writes:—

It was terrible to see the ferocity of the Ghoorkas as they sprang at their foes. They inflicted horrible wounds, but so strong are their arms, it was death every blow.

On the 19th of March, the Moosa Bagh, the last stronghold of the rebels, fell, and Lucknow was completely in our hands. Fighting still took place with large bands of rebels on the outskirts, but they were generally so demoralised that they fell an easy prey.

We cannot close this eventful chapter without detailing a gallant stand made by a slender detachment of that grand old regiment, the 42nd Black Watch. Forty-eight men of the regiment were watching a ford on the River Sardaar, which separates Oude from Rohileund. The notorious rebel Kirput Sing of Rooyat crossed at the head of 2,000 men, with two guns, and at once opened fire on the little band. They did not flinch, but stood at their post from sunrise to sunset, when two more companies came to their rescue and made their victory complete.

The enemy left 400 dead on the field, including Kirput Sing, his son and brother, along with two guns. Of the 48, five were killed and eleven wounded, including the gallant Captain Lawson.

By deeds such as these Lucknow was won, and the rebels dispersed and driven from Oude. By deeds such as these has the Empire been made, and such deeds of valour are never forgotten, but written in letters of gold on Britain's scroll of fame.

CHAPTER 3

The Fighting at Allahabad: 1857

When the spirit of revolt in our Indian Empire first spread abroad, there can be little doubt but that the minds of the mutineers were inflamed by headmen or chiefs who had a natural antipathy to Britain and everything British. We have seen how the rebels at Delhi behaved basely and treacherously, but it was the same all over the Empire. The natives in general had one common bond of union—a growing sense of distrust, and a fixed and firm apprehension that some danger menaced the religion of the Hindoo and Mohammedan alike. They were also imbued with the gross idea that either the British must be killed off root and branch throughout India, or that the followers of the Prophet or *Menou* must inevitably be swallowed up in Christianity. Anglo-Indian society remained oblivious to the threatening danger, despising the natives, and never dreaming of the power they would possess in the event of a combined mutiny.

Writing of this apathy, a writer in the *Delhi Gazette* of the time writes as follows:—

Dazzled by the brilliant facility of their past triumphs, they brought themselves to believe in a peculiar mission like the ancient Hebrews; and blindly trusting in their special Providence, neglected all ordinary human precautions for securing the safety and permanence of their position. They knew that there was an evil spirit abroad, but they took no steps to disabuse men's minds until the mischief was done. They made no preparation against the coming tempest though the sear-birds on the shore were shrilly screaming, though a black murky spot was already visible on the horizon, though the hoarse murmur of the storm was breathing heavily on the darkening waters; so, no one armed himself against the day of battle. Suddenly a spark was applied to the train laid by many hands, and in a moment of time all was death, desolation and despair.

Such undoubtedly was the case, but the native mind must have been inflamed to an extraordinary degree before the men who wore the British uniform, and who had sworn fealty to the Crown, could have descended to such vile acts of treachery as at Cawnpore and Delhi. It was at Meerut that this slumbering antipathy and racial hatred, which caused so much bloodshed and suffering first broke out. Colonel Finnis, of the 11th Native Infantry, was there shot through the back by a treacherous *sepoy*, and a hundred bayonets were plunged into his body.

This was the inauguration of the work of mutiny and blood, and all through India the spirit of antipathy animated the mutinous soldiers to deeds of Oriental barbarity. At Ferozepore, the 45th and 57th Native Infantry set the buildings on fire and committed several acts of bloodshed. At Murdaun, where the 55th Regiment (Ochterlony's men) mutinied, Colonel Spottiswoode, who loved and trusted them, was so affected that he shot himself in despair. At Allyghar, brave Captain Hayes was betrayed and hacked to pieces. At Bareilly the infuriated fanatics turned upon their officers and killed and wounded in every direction.

While at Shahjehanpore the 28th Bengal Infantry mutinied while their officers were at church. The Rev. Mr. M'Callum was shot as he ascended the pulpit, Lieutenant Spens was sabred while he knelt at prayer, Dr. Bowling was shot as he was driving his wife and child to the church, while Mr. Ricketts, the magistrate of the station, was killed in cold blood. The women and children were promised every protection, and were actually allowed to leave the station.

They were compelled to walk, and, on alighting, the fiends disregarded all their promises by bayonetting the helpless women and dashing out the brains of the children upon the ground, besides killing all the officers who had accompanied their women under the promise of protection. At Seetapore, Neemuch, Hansi, Benares and Sultanpore the same things occurred, the officers being slain without being given an opportunity to defend themselves, while the women and children and private citizens were ruthlessly massacred.

But of all the gross crimes committed during this trying time, when the flame of mutiny was spreading like wildfire through the country, there were none of such a treacherous character as that of the mutiny of the 6th Regiment of the Bengal Army at Allahabad. That regiment had fought gallantly in many a field, as its colours signified, for they bore the names "Mysore," "Bhurtpore," and "Cabul." Allahabad is a fortified city at the junction of the Ganges with the Jumna, and the fort is constructed in a strong position on a tongue of land at the confluence of the two streams.

The 6th were lying at this fort or at the cantonments as might be required, and when they heard of the mutinies at Meerut and Delhi, at once volunteered to march against the latter city. They were thanked for their offer, and the officers commanding the regiment never imagined that their men would become disaffected. A rumour became general throughout the town, however, that the regiment was about to mutiny, and what did the treacherous *sepoys* do but approach the officers, and, says a writer of the day, "with tears in their eyes entreated them to have implicit trust in their fidelity." The scene that ensued would not have disgraced the early days of the first French Revolution.

The officers and men fraternised in the most loving manner. Perfect confidence appeared to be established on both sides; but, before nightfall stragglers from other stations arrived, who worked up the credulous fools to frenzy. They were told that the Christian Queen's troops were marching all over the country, destroying all who refused to become Christians. The soldiers had been wavering, and very little required to turn them in to perfect demons, inflamed with the one desire, namely massacre and safety in flight. That same evening, about half-past nine, while the officers were in the mess bungalow, calm in a sense of security, they were suddenly startled to hear the bugles sounding the alarm.

With blanching faces they turned out of the bungalow, but the foremost fell with a bullet in his brain, and the work of mutiny had commenced. The mutineers rushed about like veritable demons, slaying and killing whoever dared to impede them. The officers made a gallant attempt to reach the shelter of the fort at the riverside, and a few actually managed to elude the maddened mutineers, but fourteen officers, including nine young ensigns of the 6th, were brutally massacred, and their bodies subjected to terrible maltreatment.

A detachment of the 6th, with two guns, was posted at the pontoon bridge to stop the progress of the mutineers from Benares, who were expected to come to Allahabad. A garden midway between that point and the fort was occupied by about 150 men of the Oude Irregular Cavalry, under Lieutenant Alexander, who was posted there for the same purpose.

When the men of the 6th at the bridge heard the sound of the bugles, they at once divined the cause, and turned the two guns in the direction of the city, also firing upon the artillery officer, who bravely dashed off amidst the shower of bullets to warn Alexander of his danger.

Meanwhile the officers of the detachment managed to effect their escape in the dark, although they were repeatedly shot at. Lieutenant Alexander, getting together as many men as could saddle, same dashing up, sword in hand, but was shot through the heart by one of the rebels. The artillery officer, being unsupported, saw that his life was in jeopardy, turned his horse, and galloped to the fort. The garrison of the fort consisted of about 70 European invalids, the Sikh Ferozepore regiment to the number of about 400, about 80 *sepoys* of the mutinous 6th regiment, along with a number of European volunteers from the city. It was out of the question to trust the men of the 6th, so the officers at once disarmed them, and found that, contrary to orders, they had loaded their rifles, which no doubt they intended to use upon the officers. They were turned out in an unarmed state, and joined their infuriated comrades in the streets of the town.

The mutineers, after looting and wrecking the cantonments, proceeded in a body to the great prison, where they easily overpowered the guards and forced an entrance. Indian prisons at the time were generally crammed full of thieves and vagabonds who could well and fitly be classed "the greatest scum on earth," and the great prison of Allahabad was no exception to the rule. The mutineers released them speedily, and the prisoners were nothing loth to join the *sepoys* in the work of havoc and death. There were about 3,000 prisoners released, and, along with the soldiers, they marched through the streets, and carried death and destruction on their march. Captain Birch, the adjutant of the fort, and Lieutenant Innes of the Engineers, chanced to be outside when the mutiny happened, and they were caught by the rebels and shot.

A worse fate befell an officer of the 6th, who chanced to fall alive into the hands of the savages—for such undoubtedly the soldiers had become. He was pinned to the earth by bayonets and a fire kindled round his body, and thus he was slowly roasted to death as his own men danced around him and mocked his agony. The European residents who chanced to fall into the hands of the mutineers were horribly outraged before death mercifully released them from their tortures.

At least fifty white men and women perished in their houses or on the streets. Some were cut to pieces by slow degrees, the nose, ears, lips, and fingers being first cut off, and then, the limbs hacked off by the *tulwars* of the rebels. An entire family was burned alive, and little children were destroyed before the eyes of agonised parents. Houses were wrecked, and choice articles either carried off or destroyed in the maddest spirit of destruction and hate.

Five officers had reached the shelter of the fort by swimming the Ganges, and three of them were in a state of nudity. The little garrison lay under arms in the fort for five days and nights, watching the infuriated *sepoys* rushing hither and thither, maddened and desperate, many of them being under the influence of the native spirit called "*Chang*," which seems to steal away any little sense the ordinary *sepoy* may have.

The big guns in the fort were brought to bear upon bands of rebels who ventured too near, and many were killed in this way, while the sharpshooters on the walls picked off a number who came within range.

The city volunteers, composed for the most part of railroad men, were formed into three small companies and officered. This added to the numerical strength of the garrison, and Colonel Neill at Benares, hearing of the outbreak at Allahabad, sent on about 50 men of the Madras Fusiliers, while he himself hurried to the scene of the mutiny at the head of 40 more, covering the seventy miles of country which lay between the two cities in two nights in light carriages. He found on arrival at Allahabad that the mutineers had grown tired of looting and killing, in fact, the 6th had marched out of the town with drums beating.

Neill, at the head of his fusiliers, speedily cleared the suburbs, and had for his opponent a Mohammedan *Mollah*, who had unfurled the green flag of the Prophet and proclaimed himself Vice-Regent of the King of Delhi. He had collected a large band of ruffians, and occupied an entrenched position in the town. At the head of only 200 men, with a few guns, Neill marched out of the fort and attacked the *Mollah's* forces so suddenly, and with such vigour, that the rebels broke and fled in all directions, pursued by the energetic Fusiliers, who put many to death.

Meanwhile, the scene inside the fort was a sad one, cholera breaking out, and many also perished from sunstroke. Over seventy fighting men lost their lives through disease, and twenty were buried at one funeral.

The shrieks of the insane and the dying rang through the fort, and the 200 fugitive European women were in a sad plight. However, when once Neill with his small force got thoroughly to work in the streets, he rapidly cleared the rebels out of the city, and the fugitives were able to return to their wrecked homes. The mortality was very high for a time, but gradually the disease got stamped out, and Allahabad became free and latterly welcomed Sir Henry Havelock and his Highlanders on their march to Lucknow.

CHAPTER 4

The Fighting at Futtehghur: 1857

The 10th Native Infantry, while the foregoing events were occurring, were stationed at Futtehghur, a town on the west bank of the Ganges. This regiment was every whit as famous in Indian warfare as the 6th, who had run amok at Allahabad, bearing on their colours the Battles of Buxar and Korah.

In June, 1857, the whole regiment broke out into open mutiny, forced the gaol and released all the prisoners. This was surprising in the extreme, as only a few days previous the men of the 10th had informed their officers of a plan which the 41st regiment at Seetapore had proposed to them in the event of the mutiny. They had even gone the length of destroying the pontoon bridge, so as to prevent any rebels from crossing to Futtehghur. No sooner did the 41st arrive after their mutiny at Seetapore, than the 10th regiment, with a company of artillery and two guns, marched to the *Nawab*, whom they placed on the throne, laying the British colours at his feet, and firing a salute of 21 guns.

The battalion of the 10th were split into two sections, those who were Purbees crossing at once to Oude, with the obvious intention of returning to their homes. They were accompanied by a Captain Bignell, who was killed on the way. Others went off on foraging expeditions in small bands, and many who remained were murdered by the men of the 41st, because the men of that regiment were refused a share of the public treasure.

The garrison at Futtehghur was but a small one, in fact there were only about thirty men capable of bearing arms, and these brave fellows prepared to defend the seventy odd women and children against the attacks of the mutineers. The forces exchanged shots with big guns, and latterly the *sepoys* crept behind the sheltering bushes, and peppered the defenders with a heavy musketry fire, which did no harm.

On the following day the persistent rebels, under cover of their artillery fire, were seen approaching with ladders, which they attempted to set up against the walls. Fortunately, the men inside the fort were good marksmen, and were successful in shooting down the bearers of the ladders as they approached.

For four consecutive days the enemy's guns and rifles continued to play upon the fort, and there were several ineffectual attempts to scale the walls. The rebels adopted a new plan on the fifth day, as the riflemen took up positions on the roofs of houses within range. This fire was most deadly, and four of the little garrison were wounded. They next loopholed the walls, and kept up at steady fire at any of the garrison who showed his head above the wall to fire the cannon. Mr. Jones and Colonel Tucker were killed in this manner. On the following day, Conductor Aherne, with one single discharge of grape, was successful in blowing a dozen of the rebels away from the wall of a woodyard.

The rebels then fell into a trap, for after they had cut a hole into this place, the defenders allowed them to enter one by one. When a sufficient number were in, a well-directed shot was thrown amongst them, doing great damage. The place was then set on fire about their ears, and many perished. Frustrated in this attempt, the rebels now commenced a mine, at which they worked in secret for two nights and then sprung it. The report was awful, and the fort was shaken to its very foundations, but no lives were lost.

A breach was, however, made in the walls, and the *sepoys* were preparing to escalade it, when they were forced to retire under a heavy musketry fire, through which they lost several men. Later in the day they made a second attempt, with no better result, although the garrison lost one of its best gunners in the person of Conductor Aherne, who was shot through the head in laying a gun.

Maddened by such frequent failure, and eager to get at the garrison for the purpose of massacre, the mutineers got a gun into position, and started to fire upon the bungalow which they knew contained the women and children. A number of shots passed through the door, but extra precautions had been hurriedly taken, and the balls were stopped by a heavy timber barricade. Two of the enemy's guns were dismounted, but still the rebels kept up the attack upon the wearied garrison, and, finding all their attempts useless, started to sink a second mine close to the position of the first. This was a serious outlook, for if a second breach was made, the rebels would make two different attacks, and the defenders were too few to repel the rebels in large numbers at two different places.

They looked for a means of escape, and the only possible way that presented itself was the river, which flowed past the fort. They could not stay in the fort, for it simply meant that sooner or later they would be all savagely butchered, so the brave men who had guarded the women and children so faithfully and well, determined that under cover of night they would make the attempt. The ladies and children were divided into three parties, and at midnight they silently quitted the fort in which they had spent so many anxious and perilous nights. Quickly they took their places in the respective boats, and then an officer went round to call in the pickets, who had previously spiked the guns and destroyed the ammunition.

At two o'clock on the morning of the 4th July, the fugitives shoved off, and congratulated themselves in making their escape unobserved. They could not foresee the end, nor could they rend the veil and know the dreadful fate that was in store for them. The *sepoys* had not their eyes shut, for no sooner had the boats passed the walls of the fort than the cry rang out, "The *Feringhees* are escaping." They ran along the bank, firing at the boats, which fortunately were out of range, and the fugitives had gone down the river about a mile without mishap when it was found that the boat which contained Colonel Goldie, his wounded daughter, and other delicate sufferers was too heavy to be managed, so all the occupants had to be transferred to the boat under the command of Colonel Smith. This was safely accomplished, although the *sepoys* brought a cannon into play. The boats proceeded down midstream, with the *sepoys* in attendance, shouting and firing from the bank.

At the village of Singheerampore they had to lie-to to repair a broken rudder, and two men were killed by a shot from the bank. Further misfortune was in store for the fugitives, as the other boat grounded on a sandbank, and all the efforts of the men to move her failed. A panic seized the occupants of the craft, and when two boatloads of *sepoys* were seen approaching, the women and children became frantic, and when the *sepoys* opened fire, they threw themselves into the water rather than fall into the murderous hands of the *sepoys*. All the ladies were soon struggling in the water, with the exception of a Mrs. Fitzgerald, who remained in the boat with her child, while her husband stood over her with musket loaded and bayonet fixed. A few of the occupants of the boat escaped by swimming to the other boats.

Those who were in the other boats were scarcely less unfortunate, for the *sepoys* poured in a merciless fire of grape shot among the women and children. Mr. Jones, who swam to another boat, found most of the occupants dead—a Mr. Rohan, the younger Miss Goldie, a child and another lady lying in the bottom of the boat. All through the night the survivors of the Futtehghur garrison continued their perilous voyage, ever and *anon* hearing the shouts of their pursuers and the constant drip of the bullets in the turgid waters.

They passed Bithoor, where they were fired upon by the *sepoys* under that infamous scoundrel Nana Sahib. The fire was deadly, and many were wounded. The boats still proceeded down the river, and at last reached Cawnpore, where General Wheeler received them. They had been but spared from one death to another equally as horrible, for they received no mercy from the *Nana*, and, as described in the chapter dealing with Cawnpore, were brutally massacred. The bravery of the defenders at Allahabad and Futtehghur are bright incidents in a campaign which was distinguished for bravery.

CHAPTER 5

The Siege of Kotah: 1858

We have now to deal with perhaps the most sanguinary conflict which marked the closing days of the campaign, when British arms were employed in stamping out the mutiny in all directions. Sir Hugh Rose was entirely successful in Central India, General Whitlock cleared the whole district of Jubbulpore, white General Roberts, sweeping through Rajpootana, bore down upon Kotah, the inhabitants of which had cruelly massacred the Resident, Major Burton, and his two sons.

Kotah is in the province of Ajmere, and was held by the noted rebel, Hossein Ali, who had gathered around him a large force to make a stand against the all-conquering *Feringhees*. It was in March, 1858, that Roberts commenced his movement upon Hossein Ali, and a trying tramp it proved for his brave troops. Under a sweltering sun, over baked earth, finding the wells dried up, with men and horses dropping by the way, he wearily dragged his way toward Kotah. To add to the sufferings of his troops, most of the water-carriers deserted to the ranks of the rebel chief, and left the British soldiers parched and thirsty.

The column consisted of the 8th Royal Irish Hussars, the 72nd, or Duke of Albany's Highlanders, the 83rd and 95th regiments, along with the 13th Bengal Infantry—a corps which was greatly mistrusted. The enemy consisted almost entirely of mutineers, chiefly of the 72nd Bengal Infantry, whose scarlet coats were faced with yellow, like those of the 72nd Highlanders who were marching against them, while they also bore the same number on all their appointments as the British regiment.

Bravely the force marched on, passing on the route Sawoor, which was strongly fortified; Jhajpoor, a straggling ill-defended town; and Bhoondee. This latter place is a national citadel, and it was here that the two brigades met, being only two days' march from Kotah.

On the 22nd of March, the division, after great hardships, reached Kotah, and encamped on the left bank of the River Chumbul, opposite the city, but this position had ultimately to be altered to avoid the enemy's artillery. The whole army lay exactly opposite the city, and parallel with the river. The immediate cause of these operations against Kotah was the treachery of the *rajah*, who had always protested himself a staunch ally of the British.

When the mutiny at Neemuch broke out among the Bengal troops, Major Burton had left Kotah for some purpose. During his absence, the Rajah warned him against returning, as the inhabitants had joined the rebellion, and considerable numbers of mutineers had taken up their residence in the city. Nevertheless, Major Burton, with his two sons, returned to Kotah, and all three were barbarously murdered. The *rajah* refused to join his subjects, and shut himself up in his palace, where he was regularly besieged by his own subjects.

Kotah is a large town, girt by massive walls, and is situated on the eastern bank of the Chumbul, well defended by bastions and deep ditches cut in the solid rock, while the entrances are all defended by double gates. In the foreground lies a vast lake, with the temple of Jugmandal built of snow-white marble, rising in the centre.

On the 24th of March two batteries were erected on the banks of the river, one on the right and the other on the left of the British position. Hossein Ali, who was in reality an ex-pay sergeant of the revolted 72nd, had about 70 pieces of cannon at his disposal, and he directed a well-trained fire upon the batteries. The siege began with vigour, and the guns of both forces did much execution. Night and day our soldiers and officers toiled in a trench on the scheme of a mine, which was afterwards relinquished, amid slaughter, wounds, sunstroke, and cholera, but they never flinched.

On the 26th, Major-General Roberts placed a body of troops in the entrenched quarter of the city, which was still in the possession of the *rajah*, while 200 men of the 83rd regiment, and the rifle company of the 13th Native Infantry, crossed over the river. The next day or two, during which the artillery fire on both sides never slackened, was given over to preparations for bringing over some of the heavy ordnance and mortars to be used in a grand assault.

On the 30th the final preparations were made, and early that morning three columns of 500 men each passed over in large square flat-bottomed boats to the city, the reserve being under Colonel Macan. The leading column in the assault, under the command of

Lieut.-Colonel Raimes of the 95th, was composed of 260 men of the 72nd, and 250 of the 13th Native Infantry; the second column, under Lieut.-Colonel Holmes of the 12th Native Infantry, of 260 men of the 95th regiment, with the 10th regiment of Native Infantry; and the third column of 200 of the 83rd, with the 12th Native Infantry.

The Highlanders crept up to the wall in the early morning while it was yet dark, the design being to blow a hole in the wall sufficiently large to admit a storming party. The engineers found the wall too solid to admit of its being blown up. The engineers toiled away, but the day broke and the sun shone forth making conspicuous the Highlanders in their plumed bonnets and tartan trews as they stood in line under the wall of the city. They became exposed to a galling fire from the enemy, and their position for a time was a most dangerous one.

The plan of attack was altered, and the 72nd, with the engineers and supports, were ordered to the Kittenpole gate, which, although it had been strongly built up, presented more favourable opportunities for capture. The engineers set to work, and in a few minutes, they had the ponderous gate blown to atoms.

Under a heavy fire the 72nd, under Major Thelluson, dashed in at the breach, and won an entrance to the city by turning to the right under the protecting fire of a party which had been placed on the walls of the *rajah's* fortifications. The advance was rapid, as nothing could stay the impetuous rush of the Highlanders, who were smarting under the heavy fire they had been subjected to in the morning. It was a fearful moment for them while they stood under the walls, waiting for an entrance, and one of the regiment wrote home as follows:—

We were in an awful position for more than seven hours. I think it would be about eleven o'clock when the gate was up. But it was too bad to keep us in suspense so long, for you may believe me the torture of the mind was awful. Any who had the opportunity of studying the men's countenances could easily read their minds. You would have seen many a shade of sorrow and sadness. Our plan of attack was simple. Our brigade—the second—was to attack and storm the right bastions, mounting in all 17 guns, the 72nd forcing through the breach first, supported by the 13th, the 83rd bringing up the rear. The first brigade was to follow on the left attack, both having the town in the centre.

To the sound of the pipes, and shouting the old war-cry of the

Greys which had resounded over the field of Waterloo—"Scotland for ever!"—the Albany Highlanders (72nd) dashed on. But little resistance was offered, and rapidly the column moved on to the chief point of attack—the bastion called the Zooraidoor, on the outer walls of the city. The rebels, with their matchlock rifles, tried in vain to stop the onslaught, but fell against the deadly Enfield rifle. On the column reaching the bastion, it was found that most of the enemy had fled, and those who remained were quickly put to flight by the bayonet. Several of the mutineers, in their haste to escape, threw themselves from the ramparts, and were dashed to pieces at the bottom.

The column next proceeded along the wall as far as the Soorjpole gate, one of the principal entrances to the town, through which a body of the enemy were flying to a place of safety.

Then commenced the real fighting of the day, for when the column had seized the gate and rushed into the city, the rebels opened a heavy fire upon the British when they had quitted the shelter of the walls. They were entrenched in a strongly-fortified house facing the gateway, which was stormed by Lieutenant Cameron of the 72nd with a handful of men. Cheering and shouting, they rushed in amongst the hail of bullets, and dashed up a narrow passage and staircase leading into the upper part of the building, where they met with a determined resistance from the rebels. The band was headed by "*the Lalla*," the commander-in-chief of the mutineers, who fought desperately.

Lieutenant Cameron was cut down, and several men were killed, so Lieut.-Colonel Parke deemed it expedient to risk no more lives in a fight in the narrow, dark, and intricate passages of the building. The Royal Engineers were told off to destroy the building, and they soon exploded their powder bags at the corner of the building, bringing it down like a house of cards. A large number of the rebels were destroyed by the collapse of the building, while those who sought safety in the open were cut down. There were a few instances of desperate resistance but the rout was complete.

The other two columns operating at different points met with scarce a check, for the rebels made every haste to save their skins. By evening the whole strongly-fortified city of Kotah was in our hands, and the slaughter of the rebels must have been severe. The 8th Hussars gallantly charged after the flying mutineers, and cut down hundreds of them, capturing the treasure which had been taken from the town, while the 72nd Highlanders captured one stand of *sepoy* colours, and the 95th two stands. The victory was really gained by a clever flank movement, coupled with the fact that the rebels deserted their guns, which, had they been as well handled as in the early morning, would have repelled any attack.

Upwards of 70 guns of different calibre, some very heavy, and a vast quantity of ammunition, fell into our hands. General Roberts, in thanking the brigade, said that he had been in field fights, he had been in storming parties, but he had never seen men go steadier. It was more like men upon a parade, or on a field day, than men who were facing death. Thus ended the siege of Kotah, which will be for ever memorable for British bravery against terrible odds.

CHAPTER 6

The Fighting at Jhansi, Rohan, and Bareilly: 1857–58

One of the many black deeds of the mutiny was the inhuman atrocities at Jhansi, in the province of Allahabad, and about a hundred miles eastward of Serinje. In June, 1857, the 12th Native Infantry, which had served with distinction at Ferozeshah, and the 14th Irregular Cavalry had their headquarters at Nowgong, but the left wing of each regiment was quartered at Jhansi, which had therefore a considerable force to repel any attack, besides having the advantage of two forts for defensive purposes.

The spirit of mutiny was in the air, and although the regiments named had remained true to their salt, their officers could not put implicit trust, in them in face of the stories which were being circulated regarding the success of the mutineers in various parts of India. The officers and women and children took possession of the fort in the city, it being preferred to the Star Fort, which was in the cantonments. For a time, the *sepoys* remained true, but on the 4th of June a company of the 12th Native Infantry entered the Star Fort, and took possession of the cannon and treasure which it contained. The fat was now in the fire, and although the remainder of the men assured the poor isolated officers that they would remain faithful, no trust could be reposed in them.

In all the phases of the mutiny the crafty and cunning traits in the Indians' character were brought to the surface. They behaved treacherously on every occasion, and broke vows which to them ought to have been sacred. It was thus at Jhansi, and the officers found that they were indeed in perilous straits. On the 5th of June, while on parade, the men, who were still allowed to retain their rifles, deliberately shot down Captain Dunlop and Ensign Taylor, and Lieutenant Campbell was seriously wounded, but succeeded in escaping to the fort. Lieutenant Turnbull took refuge in the branches of a tree, but was brought down by a musket ball, and shared the same fate as Dunlop and Taylor. The other officers who were in the fort at the time of the outbreak, saw what was happening by the aid of field glasses.

They at once put themselves on the defensive, and after admitting Campbell to the shelter of the fort, secured the gates and shot down a few of the mutineers who had pursued the wounded officer. They barricaded the gates with stones, and prepared to fight desperately for their lives. There were only 55 Europeans in the place, including the women and children, along with a number of native servants. The women as usual showed admirable bravery and fortitude, cooking for the garrison, carrying refreshments to them at great risk, and, when ammunition became scarce, they cast bullets for the rifles.

The native servants were even not to be trusted, and two of them were discovered attempting to open the gates of the fort. Captain Burgess shot one of the rascals, but the other managed to cut down Lieutenant Powys before he was shot by the captain. The mutineers gathered in force around the little fort, and kept up a heavy fire upon the walls with cannon and musket. Twice the brave defenders attempted to send word of their peril to Gwalior or Nagode, but both failed. Captain Gordon was shot in the head while looking over the parapet of the fort, and as ammunition and provisions were almost exhausted, the little garrison began to lose heart.

The rebels were most persistent in their attacks, and a further disaster befell the brave defenders when two gates were battered in. The rebels offered them their lives if they laid down their arms, and as the days passed and no sign of relief came, the wearied officers were compelled at last to throw themselves upon the mercy of the mutineers. They accordingly came out of the fort and laid down their arms. The mutinous troops at once threw themselves upon the now defenceless men, and tied them in two rows.

The men were the first victims of the massacre, Captain Burgess taking the lead, his elbows tied behind his back, and a prayer book in his hands. The women and children, terrified at the murder of those near and dear to them, stood by and calmly waited until the time came when they too would be despatched. Not one escaped, but fortunately all were destroyed without the inhuman indignities to which they were subjected elsewhere.

It was left to Sir Hugh Rose, latterly Lord Strathnairn, to avenge this black deed. On the 21st March, 1858, he arrived before the walls of the city with a large force, to find that it was held by a large rebel army. He commenced the bombardment of the town, but was immediately brought face to face with a new danger. The Gwalior contingent, which had been shattered, and was thought to be dispersed, advanced from Kalpee, a town on the right bank of the Jumna, and, becoming largely augmented as it marched, the force when it drew up to give battle to Sir Hugh Rose's troops, must have numbered 25,000, while it was also supported by eighteen large pieces of artillery. Still, it was not a disciplined force, and Sir Hugh was quick to avail himself of this fact. Without giving the rebels time to form any preconcerted plan, he dashed out to the attack.

So sudden was the onslaught and so daring in its conception, the huge mass of rebels reeled and broke into a confused rout. The British, with a ringing cheer, charged in amongst the now terrified rebels, and the slaughter was great. The contingent was again dispersed, and fully 2,000 were killed. All the guns, elephants, and ammunition fell into our hands, and Sir Hugh was now able to resume his siege operations on the town. The rebels in Jhansi must have been affected by the defeat of the large force outside, for on the following day the town fell into the hands of the British column, the garrison fleeing in the course of the night. The pursuit was at once taken up, and before it ended 1,500 of the rebels who had been concerned in the Jhansi revolt were destroyed. This was one of the last acts in the mutiny, but the revolt was not to be quelled without the spilling of more British blood in the ill-planned attack on Roohea.

The Highland Brigade, after the final relief and capture of Lucknow, had been engaged in pursuing the rebels in the district and stamping out the rebellion in the province. The Highlanders were encamped at the Dalkoosha, having been ordered to form part of the Rohilcund field force under Brigadier Walpole. On the morning of the 8th of April, the 42nd, 79th, and 93rd Highlanders marched from the camp to the Moosha Bagh, a short distance from which the brigade encamped.

Here they remained until the 15th, when orders were issued to recommence the march, as it had been learned that the enemy were active in the vicinity. The advance guard consisted of three companies of the Black Watch with cavalry and guns, under the command of Major Wilkinson, while the main body followed with the remainder of the 42nd leading. The Highland Brigade was under the command of Brigadier the Hon. Adrian Hope, the whole being under Walpole.

Long before daylight on the 16th the force was under arms, and moved cautiously a few miles across country, when a halt was called, the baggage collected, and a strong guard set over it, consisting of two guns and detachments of men from every regiment. About ten o'clock in the morning the whole force advanced cautiously through some thick wood, and came suddenly upon a native mud fort, the garrison of which immediately opened fire with their heavy guns and musketry. The 42nd was in advance, supported by the 93rd, the 79th being held in reserve.

The guns were quickly placed in position, and opened a heavy fire upon the fort, while a movement was also made by the infantry, the Highlanders advancing under a merciless shower of bullets close to the walls of the fort. This mud erection, which did duty as a fort, was called Roohea, and was hardly worth the attention of the British troops. Walpole, however, was determined to clear out this neat of rebels, and gave orders that the infantry were to approach as near the enemy as they could, and skirmish without support.

The British plans were decidedly bad, for the rebels could easily have been driven out by the fixed bayonet without the sacrifice of life which a skirmishing attack entailed. Walpole evidently meant to prevent the escape of the rebels by the main gate, for Major Wilkinson made an attack on the weak side to drive the rebels out and into contact with the main force. Captain Ross Grove, with No. 8 Company of the Black Watch, advanced with fixed bayonets, and without having the slightest protection or cover bravely marched on till they came close to the counterscarp of the ditch, with only the breadth of the ditch between the gallant Highlanders and the enemy.

There they lay, waiting patiently for orders to charge, losing men rapidly; in fact, so precarious was their position that a company of the Punjaub Rifles was sent to their assistance. The Punjaubees and Highlanders quickly forming into line, rushed for the ditch, and attempted to get over the parapet, but had to admit defeat, having to retire with heavy loss, two officers and fifty men being killed and wounded. The impetuous assault had failed, and the enemy had sustained but a trifling loss, while the fort was as stoutly defended as ever.

Captain Cope, of the Punjaub Rifles, along with four men of the Black Watch, performed a daring deed in going almost under the walls of the fort to bring in the dead body of Lieutenant Willoughby. Creeping to where the lieutenant's body lay, the five men raised it and carried it back to the British lines under a perfect storm of shot. Captain Cope had his left arm broken by a bullet, and Private Spence, of the 42nd, was mortally wounded.

Brigadier Adrian Hope, angry at the heavy loss inflicted on his men, went near the fort to reconnoitre and endeavour, if possible, to find a better way by which it could be won. The fort was hexagonal in shape, with two redoubts, two sides of the hexagon having no fortifications. The bastions were circular, and the ditch deep and narrow, the escarp and rampart being completely inaccessible at most parts without the use of scaling ladders.

The gallant leader of the Highlanders, in his eagerness to learn the internal arrangements, ventured too near, and he had barely been a minute in the zone of fire when he was seen to sway and fall. The bullet had penetrated above the left collar-bone, and he knew that it was mortal, for he exclaimed, "I am a dead man, lads. They have done for me at last." He then asked for a drink of water, which he drank hurriedly, and then expired in the arms of one of his officers.

An officer, writing of the scene, says:—

I cannot describe to you the gloom—thick and palpable—which the sudden and untimely death of our amiable and gallant brigadier has cast over the minds of all. He was the foremost and most promising of all the young brigadiers; he was the man in whom the commander-in-chief placed the most implicit confidence, and whom all trusted and delighted to honour.

He was the ninth son of the Earl of Hopetoun, and served with the 60th Scottish Rifles in the Kaffir war, where he saw much service. No. 8 Company of the Black Watch were maddened by this loss, and retired clamouring for orders to storm the fort, but appealed in vain, for apparently Walpole had different plans in view. The same writer above quoted states:—

Everybody asks what did the brigadier intend to do? Why did he send men to occupy the position which they did when nothing was to be gained by their being there? Why, if he intended to take the place, was it not stormed at once, and at the point of the bayonet? Or rather—and this is the main query—why was it not shelled by the mortars and smashed by the breaching cannon?

For an hour or two the guns played on the fort, but after the death of Hope nothing was done, and the force outside continued to get the worst of it. All the regiments were losing heavily, but it was the Black Watch and the Punjaubees who suffered most severely, the Black Watch having alone forty-two casualties, including Lieutenants Douglas and Bromley.

At sunset the force was withdrawn, and, to the amazement of all, the camp was formed within a mile of the fort, the rebels firing upon the force as it retired. Next morning, when the men moved up to recommence the attack, it was found that the enemy had retired during the night, leaving nothing behind but the ashes of their dead, and a broken gun carriage. Quietly, thinking no doubt of their dead comrades who had perished in making the assault upon such a paltry place, the Highlanders took possession of the fort, and it was soon given over to the flames.

It was found that it was so open and unprotected behind that a regiment of cavalry could have ridden in; and yet the brave Highlanders, who were eager and willing to rush in with their trusty bayonets, were held back, and became targets for a foe concealed behind the brown walls. The garrison was only 400 strong, and the rebels could not have lost many men. A writer says:—

A sad, sad scene it was, the burial of our dead on the evening of the following day.

A short distance from the camp, in a cluster of mango trees, the graves were dug, and the slain consigned to them. The Church of England service was read by a chaplain of that church, and afterwards there was a short service, consisting of the reading of a portion of Scripture, a short address, and lastly prayers. Thus, Adrian Hope was left to sleep with the brave men who had fallen in such a miserable engagement as the taking of the mud fort of Roohea.

The rebels had to be pursued, however, and throwing sentiment to the winds, the force moved away on the 17th, and three days afterwards came up to the enemy at the village of Allahgunge. They were in large numbers, and, after the success at Roohea, they were prepared to fight desperately. The British were just as eager to come to grips, and although the rebels were strongly posted, the attack was too much for them. Burning with a desire for revenge, the Highlanders threw themselves upon the enemy, who stoutly met the onslaught. There was a wavering in the ranks when the bayonets flashed, and almost without having the opportunity of firing a shot, the enemy broke and dispersed in all directions, leaving a large number of killed and wounded upon the field.

The force stayed at Allahgunge for three days, occupied in rebel-hunting, while reinforcements also arrived. The next point was an extensive drive in the direction of Bareilly and Shahjehanpoor, and, on 5th May, after a fortnight's marching, by which the district was almost, cleared, the force once more came into contact with an extensive band of rebels on the plains to the east of Bareilly.

The engagement was a most trying one, the day being tremendously hot, but the soldiers kept up wonderfully well, and after fighting for about four hours, forced the enemy to retire with some loss. The city of Bareilly was then taken possession of, the victorious troops meeting with but slight opposition, although the 93rd lost several men in a skirmish with a band of rebels who had taken refuge in one of the buildings in the town. The mutineers were now thoroughly cowed, and the Highlanders kept them continually on the move, dispersing several bands who had attempted to rally. The 93rd marched to Shahjehanpoor, to form a brigade with the 60th Rifles and 66th Ghoorkas. Along with, this force were some guns, baggage, cavalry, and a few irregulars.

The rebels were first of all encountered at a village named Poosgawah, in which they were strongly entrenched. From this position they were quickly expelled, and the force breaking up into small parties started in pursuit of the retreating mutineers. No sooner had the bulk of the force passed through the village than a body of rebel cavalry appeared in the rear and attacked the baggage as it was straggling through the narrow entrance to the village. The main body of the baggage guard was far in the rear, and the enemy was at first mistaken for the irregulars of the force until they began to cut up the camp followers.

At this moment the sick of the 93rd, twelve in number, who, at Surgeon Munro's request, had been armed the night before, turned out of their *dhoolies* and kept up a sharp fire, which held the enemy in check until the arrival of the Mooltanee cavalry, which had been sent from the front, and which dispersed the rebels at the second charge, the men wielding their heavy cavalry swords with great dexterity, and doing considerable execution amongst the mutineers.

The British force did not suffer much loss, chiefly camp followers, but the bravery of the wounded Highlanders undoubtedly saved the situation. The force remained in the vicinity of the village for a few days, and then once more got into grips with the rebels, who were found in position at a village called Russelpoor, on the opposite side of a deep *nullah*, flanked on one side by a large village, and on the other by some rising ground.

The guns and the 6th Rifles attacked, the main body of the 93rd being held in reserve, one company, under Captain M'Bean, supporting the heavy guns. The rebels fought with grim determination, and doggedly stuck to their posts, although they were losing heavily under the accurate British fire, the big gun doing great damage to the houses of the village.

The attack was entirely successful, and the enemy were eventually driven from their position and put to flight with considerable loss to themselves. The battle of Bareilly, in which the 42nd played so important a part, opened with a short cannonade for about half an hour, the enemy who had gathered in large numbers, latterly falling back from the bridge and *nullah*, and occupied the clumps of trees and ruined houses in the cantonments.

In this position it was necessary to shell every clump and house before advancing, which caused considerable delay. All the time the sun was beating down fiercely upon the troops. About ten in the morning the enemy made a bold attempt to turn the British left flank, and the 42nd were ordered forward in support of the 4th Punjaub Rifles, who had been sent to occupy the old cavalry lines, but were there surprised by the enemy in great numbers. Just as the 42nd reached the old lines they were met by the Punjaubees in full flight, followed by a band of Ghazees brandishing their *tulwars* and shields. These rushed furiously on, and the men of the Black Watch were for a moment undecided whether they should fire upon them or not, their friends the Punjaubees being mixed up with them, when, as if by magic, the commander-in-chief appeared behind the line, and his familiar voice, loud and clear, was heard calling out, "Fire away, men! shoot them down, every man Jack of them!"

Then the line opened fine, but so desperate were the Ghazees that several of them had actually reached the line, and were about to engage the Highlanders when they were swept aside by the volley which spurted in one flame from the ranks. Four of the Ghazees seized Colonel Cameron in the rear of the line, and would have dragged him off his horse, when Colour-Sergeant Gardiner rushed from the ranks and bayoneted them, the colonel escaping with only a slight wound on the wrist. For this act of bravery Gardiner was deservedly decorated with the Victoria Cross.

The enemy now fell back under the fire of the Highlanders, who were at last given the order to advance with fixed bayonets. The rebels had had enough, and broke and fled, leaving the 42nd and 79th to take possession of the fort and post a line of pickets from the fort to the extreme right of the commander-in-chief's camp.

The rebels' power was now completely broken, and they were harried from place to place, receiving no quarter unless they voluntarily surrendered. The famous Highland Brigade, comprising the Black Watch, 78th, and 93rd regiments, were ordered to stay at Bareilly, and during a particularly hot month so far as weather was concerned, took part in many expeditions against the rebels who made any show of resistance. A private writing home at this time says:—

What a change has come over the enemy. At Lucknow and Cawnpore, they were as brave as lions, but now I question if they have as much of that quality as the mouse. We are engaged in 'rebel-hunting,' and find the constant knocking about very trying. We have not had a really good brush with the enemy for weeks. Whenever they see us, they give a long-drawn howl, and flee in all directions. We then start to ferret, them out of the brush, and poor specimens of humanity we find them. They are nothing like the fierce *sepoys* we met at the commencement of this great campaign; but no wonder, for any nation in the world would have had the spirits knocked out of them had they received half the defeats that the rebels here have had served to them. The most of them are glad to come into our lines and get a decent meal, so you can have an idea of the present state of affairs.

It was ever so, and although it took time to completely stamp out the insurrection, Bareilly was really the last engagement of any note in the mutiny, and slowly but surely the British soldier, willing and stern of purpose, traversed the land and subdued the rebellious spirits. A few chiefs showed signs of resistance for a time, and the troops were mostly engaged in expeditions against the foolish people who were now espousing a forlorn cause.

Thus, in little over a year, the rebellion which boded so ill for British rule was practically stamped out, and the massacres of the innocent avenged. Brave Sir Colin Campbell was raised to the peerage, assuming the title of Lord Clyde, and no man could grudge him the honour.

CHAPTER 7

The Capture of Canton: 1857

On the 8th October, 1856, a party of Chinese, in charge of an officer, boarded the *lorcha* or *junk Arrow*, in the Canton River, tore down the flag, and carried away the Chinese crew.

Now, the *Arrow* had not long before been registered as a British vessel, and, moreover, the outrage was carried out in defiance, not only of the master of the ship, but also of the British consul, to whom appeal was first made. In either case, the reply was the same—that the vessel was not British, but Chinese.

The fact is that for a long time past British influence in China had been on the decline. The incident of the *Arrow* constituted its first outward expression. Now, the Chinese Imperial Commissioner in Canton at this time was a man called Yeh. To this man a complaint was at once made, and, at the same time, Mr. Parkes, the British consul, thought fit to inform Sir John Browning and Commodore Elliot, the political and naval authorities respectively, of the occurrence.

Several days passed in futile negotiations, so that by the 23rd of the month the matter passed out of the hands of the civil authorities, owing to the repeated refusals of the Chinese Commissioner to order any redress. Admiral Seymour took action on that day (the 23rd), and seized the principal forts of Canton, holding them without any attempt at opposition. Still the Chinese preserved silence, but on the 25th an attack was made upon the British Consulate. This was repelled without much trouble, but other more serious conflicts were to follow.

In the opinion of the British administrative authorities in China, it was at this juncture deemed expedient to make the occasion one in which to require the fulfilment of long-evaded treaty obligations, and accordingly further demands were made upon Yeh, though the preliminary cause of dispute was still far from being settled.

The method of retort was as might have been expected—a silent celestial contempt of the barbarian demands, so the next move of the British entailed the bombardment of Yeh's official residence. Yeh now offered a reward of thirty dollars for the head of every Englishman, and matters at length grew serious.

A course of reprisals now ensued on both sides, and individual murders were not infrequent, but early in January an attempt was made to poison the whole British community in Hong-Kong, where, as in Canton, and indeed the whole of China, the name of Britisher was one to be spoken with contempt and loathing.

With such a state of affairs, and no decisive action on the part of our authorities, small wonder that British prestige suffered severely throughout China. Our influence at the Court of Pekin became nil, and it was feared that further inaction would have a prejudicial effect upon our influence in India, where rumours of the approaching mutiny were beginning to make themselves heard. Accordingly, in the spring of 1857, our government despatched to China, not only an expeditionary force of some 5,000 men, but also a Special High Commissioner and Ambassador to the Court of Pekin, in the person of the able Earl of Elgin.

Though due to arrive in Hong-Kong in May, Lord Elgin did not finally take up his duties there until the 20th September, for, on reaching Singapore in May, it was found that the mutiny in the north-west provinces in India was turning out to be far more serious than was at first anticipated. How serious indeed that mutiny finally became, is well known to every Britisher today, but Lord Elgin was one of the few men to foresee its extent even then. With a promptitude and energy meriting the highest praise, he diverted the whole of his China force to the seat of war, and he himself, only calling for a day or two at Hong-Kong, accompanied the Naval Brigade to Calcutta.

But it is with China, and not India, that we are at present concerned, and, as before intimated, the 20th September found Lord Elgin back again at Hong-Kong, awaiting reinforcements from Britain in place of those troops which he had taken on to India. The reduction of the city of Canton was the first object at which he aimed. With that city as a hostage, he deemed at possible to make terms at Pekin and restore British prestige.

Till the 28th October inaction prevailed, owing to lack of troops, but on that date the *Imperador* arrived, bringing the first batch of marines for the expedition. Early in November the American minister, the Russian, German, and French envoys were all at Hong-Kong in view of the general anti-foreign agitations of the Chinese. By the 10th December preparations were complete, and French and British Allied presented their ultimatum to Yeh. Meantime the island of Hainan was occupied by the Allied troops without resistance.

Yen's reply to the message of Britain and France was of a truly celestial wittiness. He totally denied the existence of the main grievance, that of the hostility of the Cantonese to foreigners, slurred over the affairs of Canton itself, and finally recommended Lord Elgin to "adopt the policy pursued by Sir George Bonham, which might, as in his case, procure him the Order of the Bath"! The occupation of the island of Hainan, however, he strongly resented.

On the 17th December, Lord Elgin embarked upon the *Furious*, the *Audacieuse* being the flagship of the French admiral, and the Allied fleets assembled at Blenheim beach, below Canton. Germany and the United States resolved to join the Allied Powers.

Writing from before Canton at this stage, Mr. George Wingrove Cook, the *Times* correspondent, says:—

> We must hope, in the interests of humanity, that when the allotted interval has expired, Yeh will yield. He has at his gates the representatives of the four great nations of the earth, . . . and they are all equally determined to tolerate no more this foolish Chinese pageant.

In the interests of humanity also, time was granted to as many inhabitants of Canton to escape a might care to avail themselves of the advantage. The floating population—a literal and not a figurative phrase, availed themselves largely of the interval, and house after house detached itself from what a moment before appeared to be solid ground, and slipped off down the river out of the way of the Allied guns. Half a million are said to have fled at this time. Twenty-three British ships of war, sloops, gunboats and the like were at this time before Canton, whilst the French fleet numbered nine. The combined armament was over 500 guns. Our total attacking land force numbered some 7,000 men.

Christmas Day passed uneventfully, the interval being occupied by the various naval and military preparations, and up to the last moment it was expected that Yeh would yield; but dawn on the 28th saw the last hope gone.

Just as the day was breaking, the hoisting of a white ensign to the main of the *Actaeon* gave the signal to open fire, and, with no crashing broadside, but steadily, one by one, the iron mouths belched forth their rain of shot and shell upon the doomed city. For twenty-seven hours without intermission the guns of the Allies poured their iron hail upon Canton, and the bombardment disclosed many strange traits of Chinese character, particularly the celestial impassivity.

Mr. Cook in one of his letters to the *Times*, wrote:—

> These, strange Chinese actually seem to be getting used to it. *Sampans* and even cargo boats are moving down the river like London lightermen in the ordinary exercise of their calling; people are coming down to the bank to watch the shot and shell fly over their heads. Many curious instances occurred, and strange sights were to be seen. A 12-pounder rocket fell short, and was burning on the ground, when a Chinaman attacked it with a flail as though it had been a living thing. Of course, it burst at last, and blew the poor fellow to pieces. In a room opening upon the river a family were taking their evening meal within 200 yards of the *Phlegethon*, which was keeping up a constant discharge of shells, which passed within a few yards of their heads. The light was so strong that the interior of the room was visible in all its details the inmates were all eating their rice as though nothing particular was happening outside. . . . All day long the *sampans* were proceeding from ship to ship, and selling fruit and vegetables to the sailors who were bombarding their city. Who can pretend to understand such a people as this?

Who, indeed? But the Chinese nature has a darker side, as we shall see later.

At times during the bombardment troops were disembarked for reconnaissance, and the general plan of the assault arranged, and after a brief exchange of musketry the East Fort was captured in this way, and shortly afterwards blown up.

As antagonists the Chinese were not found to be particularly formidable. They were in overwhelming number, it is true, and imbued with treachery, but while from a distance they would fire their *gingals*, so soon as our men approached to close quarters, they would throw down their arms and run.

During the first hours of bombardment, the movements of our troops on land took the form principally of reconnaissance, and the grand assault was reserved for the morning of Tuesday, 29th. The city by night, as seen from the ships, presented a wild and dazzling sight.

The inflammable houses caught here and there, and at times the whole place seemed enveloped by a ring of flame, while the native brigades could be seen rushing hither and thither in wild effort to quell the flames which everywhere opposed them.

At daybreak the general bombardment ceased, and from three divisions of the Allied troops the attack commenced, British troops forming the right and centre, the French taking the left. The extreme right was composed of our naval brigade. Some stiff fighting was anticipated before the city wall could be gained, and then, by the aid of scaling ladders, our men were to pour themselves into the city and carry by assault its main fortifications of Magazine Hill and Gough's Fort and a barn-like building called the Five-Storied Pagoda.

Now the attack commences. Sharp comes the order to advance at the double, and into the dense brushwood and tree-covered space that lies between them and the wall of Canton plunge fearlessly the troops of France and Britain.

Stubborn was the resistance of the Chinese. Dropping back from tree to tree, and firing from dense cover, practised troops might have delayed their enemy's advance indefinitely, but, strange to say, few men were killed at this point of the attack. Indeed, the loss of the Allies at the storming of Canton was extraordinarily insignificant, considering the huge number of their armed assailants.

On and on pressed our men, firing incessantly at the top of the high wall now appearing in front of them, and thronged with Chinese and Tartar soldiers, and all the while on the watch for any Chinese face which might show itself for an instant in the brushwood, or amongst the stunted hillocks. Here a man would throw up his shoulders with a short cough, struck through the lungs by a bullet from a Chinese *gingal*, aimed from who knew where; there a man would drop with a groan with shattered ankle or with wounded thigh. Instantly the bearers of the medical corps would fearlessly dash to his side, stretcher in hand, tenderly raise their wounded comrade, and, with swinging steps, remove him to the ships, where was the floating hospital.

Many gallant deeds were done by British and by French alike, but the *coolie* corps came in for the special commendation of Mr. Cook:—

They carried the ammunition on the day of the assault, close up to the rear of our columns, and when a cannon-shot took off the head of one of them, the others only cried, '*Ey yaw!*' and laughed, and worked away a merrily as ever.

At length, however, the wall is gained, and to the last the Chinese man the top and pour down a fire upon the party advancing with the scaling ladders. When at length it seems that we are not to be driven back by any force opposed, the hordes of Chinese and Tartar soldiers, leaping down inside the city, fled to conceal themselves behind the neighbouring houses to keep up a musket fire from there.

Major Luard is the first to gain the wall. Snatching the foremost ladder from its bearers, the gallant major scrambles up, closely followed by a Frenchman. A moment passes, and our men are swarming up in dozens, firing down upon the Chinese in the city, and rushing along the wall towards the right, where the Five-Storied Pagoda awaits them with sullen fire.

The fighting at the *pagoda* is short and sharp. Quick as thought the bayonets are out, and ere a few moments pass the Chinese and Tartar defenders are fleeing for their lives, with all the Chinaman's abhorrence of "barbarian" cold steel. The next to fall is Cough's Fort, where similar scenes are enacted, and, shortly after midday, the main defences of the city of Canton are in the hands of the Allies.

The total casualties had been slight—some 15 British and 2 Frenchmen killed; while the Chinese dead have been estimated at 200. But the capture of Canton may be said to be quite unlike the capture of any other city. The main defences, it is true, had fallen, but no formal surrender had occurred, and so for many days conflicts between victors and vanquished were of frequent occurrence.

The *Times* report says:—

> People ask, not what we are going to do next, but what the Chinese are going to do. These curious, stolid, imperturbable people seem determined simply to ignore our presence, and wait till we are pleased to go away. Yeh lives much as usual. He cut off 400 Chinese heads the other morning, and stuck them up in the south of the city.

A strange picture this, of a conquered city. The governor, whom one would naturally expect to be busied with making formal submission and arranging terms of surrender, going about his business as usual, and carrying on administration in his old barbaric way.

Very slowly and laboriously did the Allies effect some semblance of order in Canton, and in a few days the precise casualty list came to hand. The number of killed was as we previously stated, while the wounded totalled some 81 British and 32 French. Among the killed was gallant Captain Bate. At one stage of the attack upon the city wall it was found necessary to send someone forward to reconnoitre the ditch and ascertain the best position for the placing of a scaling ladder. This duty involved the crossing of a small vegetable patch which lay in front of our fellows, and which was exposed to a perfect hail of hostile bullets.

At once Captain Bate of the *Actaeon* volunteered for the dangerous mission, Captain Mann of the Engineers accompanying him. Quick as thought they dashed across the deadly patch of garden and reached the other side in safety, where they stood for a moment looking down into the ditch. A sigh of relief went up from our officers and men as they beheld the mission half accomplished, when suddenly Bate was seen to throw up his hands, and fall headlong. A Chinese bullet had found a billet in his brave heart. He never spoke nor stirred when, a few moments later, his body was recovered. This and many another tale of deeds bravely done was told during the succeeding days, when the Allies sought to restore some show of law and order in the city of Canton.

Mr. Cook's tale of a scene round the camp-fire of some of our naval brigade is too good to be missed, bearing in mind the strictness of law against looting. Says Mr. Cook:—

Never was an army kept under stricter discipline. The eccentricities of the British sailor are kept under strict repression by the provost-marshal, and if a man is found ten yards in front of the outposts, he is incontinently flogged, unless he happens to be a Frenchman. Yet somehow pig is very abundant. 'Where did you loot that pig, Jack?'—'Loot, sir? We never loots; there's an order against looting, and it's pretty strict, as we knows.'—'But how do you get all these pigs?'—'Why, d'ye see, we lights our fire? o' nights, and I think the pigs must all come to the light, and the sentries must take 'em for Chinamen and fire at 'em, for we generally finds two or three with their throats cut in the morning.'

"This was all the explanation I could get," adds Mr. Cook, with an undoubted chuckle.

New Year's Day, 1858, now arrived, was held as a gala day by the victorious army. A formal procession of the ambassadors was held to Magazine Hill, to officially "take possession of the city," while the ships in the harbour were decked from stem to stern with bunting. A royal salute at intervals frightened many Cantonese into the belief that the bombardment was recommencing.

Thus, the days passed, interspersed with military duties and the erection of huts upon the city walls for the occupation of the soldiers. Probably in spite of the strictness of the antilooting orders some "curio collecting" was indulged in by our men, and that not always with the willing consent of the Chinese. Anyway, many strange silks and furs and even jewelled ornaments found their way into the baggage of this man and the haversack of that.

At length, on the 5th January, the capture of the great Yeh himself was determined upon, and, once mooted, the project was carried out with secrecy, alacrity, and success. For not only did Yeh himself become a prisoner of the Allies on that day, but with him the lieutenant-governor of Canton and the Tartar general. The Treasury, 52 boxes of dollars, and many other rich spoils fell into our hands upon the same auspicious occasion. Early on the morning of the 5th, several bodies of British troops shouldered their way through the city, each upon its separate mission. That under Colonel Holloway proceeded straight to the palace of Peh-kwei, the acting governor of Canton, and little resistance was met with as they burst open the doors and searched room after room for the person of the acting-governor himself. Eventually the old gentleman was discovered at breakfast, and promptly, and without bloodshed, he was placed under arrest,

A truly Chinese interview passed between the old man and his captors. Asked for his keys and seals of office, he regretted exceedingly that that particular morning, of all others in the year, he should have mislaid them! He promised to make search for them, and once more expressed his regrets. Such shilly-shallying was too much for Colonel Holloway, and a whispered consultation followed. A few moments passed, and presently in marched a stout sergeant-major with an axe, which he brandished about in an ominous and terrifying manner! Like magic the missing keys were found, and the governor was removed to the British headquarters!

The scene at the capture of the Treasury was similarly typical of the peculiarities of the Chinese. Almost without resistance the place was taken possession of, the bayonet proving invaluable as a persuasive power, and the search for the city's treasury commenced.

Taking into account the fact that for six days no guard had been mounted to hinder the Chinese from removing their treasures, it was anticipated that little money would be found. Quite the reverse, however, proved to be the case. Fifty-two boxes of silver dollars, sixty-

The British Army striking the Chinese Guard st the Yamun of the Lieutenant-Governor of Canton

eight packets of solid ingots, and a whole room full of copper cash were recovered, while furs and silks and other loot was left untouched. The officer in command of the company, Captain Parke, pressed the Chinese *coolies* who had assembled outside in their hundreds into the work of removing the treasures of their own city to the British camp, and soon all was safely stored and under guard.

Meanwhile, in another part of the city, the French had succeeded in laying hands upon the Tartar general, who was found almost alone in a deserted palace, and elsewhere the hunt for Yeh was being vigorously pushed forward.

Mr. Parkes and Captain Key, receiving information that the Imperial Commissioner was in hiding in a library not far from the Tartar general's palace, proceeded thither with all haste, only to find one old man in possession of the place. After much interrogation and a mild threat or two, this individual was induced to lead the searchers to the house of the Tartar lieutenant-general. Here the doors were burst in by a party of a hundred bluejackets, and a room-to-room search commenced.

After a few moments an old man in a *mandarin's* cap and coat threw himself before the party of British officers, and protested wildly that he was Yeh, of whom they were in search, but so vigorous was his self-identification that it was promptly suspected that he was an impostor. He was therefore retained in custody while the search continued. He turned out subsequently to be the Tartar lieutenant-general himself, and was placed under arrest. A few moments later, Captain Key, hearing a sound as of persons escaping by the back of the house, hurried in that direction, and was just in time to perceive a *mandarin* of huge stature hastening along a narrow passage. Suspecting this person to be the Imperial Commissioner himself, Captain Key, without further ceremony, threw his arms round the neck of the fugitive, and proclaimed him prisoner.

It was indeed Yeh himself, very eager to escape, but without the slightest idea of defending himself or otherwise securing his desired purpose. Many papers were captured in the house, amongst them both incriminating and amusing documents.

Says Mr. Oliphant, Lord Elgin's secretary:—

I reached Magazine Hill (where the headquarters were established) shortly after the prisoners arrived there. Yeh, seated in a large room, and surrounded by some of his immediate attendants, was answering in a loud, harsh voice questions put to him by Sir Michael Seymour with reference to Englishmen who had been prisoners in his hands. Though he endeavoured, by the assumption of a careless and insolent manner to conceal his alarm, his glance was troubled, and his fingers trembled with suppressed agitation!

He had heavy sensual features, this mighty *mandarin*, whose power was such that he had caused to be beheaded no fewer than 70,000 of his countrymen during his two years of office in Canton. But though Yeh may have been in some state of perturbation while interrogated by our high officials, he yet retained sufficient self-possession to display great insolence. In the matter of the British prisoners, he was unable, he said, to recall exactly what had become of them, but, after all, it was an unimportant matter! Mr. Parkes, one of only two really competent Chinese linguists, acted as interpreter.

It was soon decided that little information could be got from Yeh, and it was determined to keep him prisoner on board the *Inflexible*, whither he was at once conveyed, under a strong guard. A few days later the Governor Peh-kwei was formally restored to his office as administrator of Pekin, with the assistance of an Allied council of three, composed of Colonel Holloway, Captain Martineau, and Mr. Parkes.

Lord Elgin, Baron Gros, and other plenipotentiaries were present at his installation, which was conducted with much pomp and ceremony. In the course of an address, Lord Elgin pointed out the firm resolve of the Allied Governments to retain military occupation of the city until such time as all questions pending between these Governments and the Emperor of China should be satisfactorily settled. In the meantime, it was intended that the governor, with the newly-appointed Council, should be responsible for the preservation of order in Canton.

Thus, for some days matters remained, while negotiations with Pekin proceeded. The time was spent in perfecting, so far as possible, the affairs of the city of Canton, meting out a rough justice, and in visiting the prisoners, where indescribable horrors and past brutalities upon the unhappy prisoners were brought to light by our commissioners. Most of the poor wretches found surviving were liberated, and a more liberal and humane policy urged upon the Chinese Government.

About this time America and Russia joined with France and Britain in the agreement to insist upon the proper recognition and treatment of foreigners throughout the Chinese Empire. The main terms insisted upon by the Allies at Pekin were the appointment of a high Chinese official to confer with Europeans upon matters concerning them, such as a free transit throughout China under proper protection from Chinese authority; permanent diplomatic relations at Pekin; unrestricted commerce, and indemnity for losses and expenses incurred.

On the satisfactory adjustment of these matters the international blockade of the port of Canton was raised on the 10th February, and in about three weeks' time Lord Elgin and Baron Gros proceeded north. The treaty of Tientsin was signed on June 26, 1858, and for a time comparative quiet prevailed in China. The British colony at Canton was re-established, and Yeh, the late Imperial Commissioner, degraded from his office, was deported by the British to India.

CHAPTER 8

The Battles at the Taku Forts: 1860

It is one thing to make a treaty with the wily Celestial, but quite another to see that that treaty is enforced.

The causes which led to the Chinese War of 1860 are soon told. Together with France, her old ally of 1858, Britain had determined to strictly enforce the stipulations of the treaty of Tientsin, which followed on the fall of Canton, but when a British envoy was entering the Peiho River for the purpose of obtaining the formal ratification of the treaty, fire was opened upon the squadron from the forts at the mouth of the river.

Thus, it was that a British Army of about 10,000 men, and a French force of 7,000 men were despatched to China. Our army, the bulk of which came from India, was collected at Hong-Kong during March and the beginning of April. It comprised two infantry divisions, a cavalry brigade, and a small siege train. The 1st Division, consisting of the 1st Royal Scots, the 2nd (Queen's), the 31st, and the 60th (Rifles) regiments of British soldiers, the 15th Punjaub Infantry, and the Loodianah regiments of native Indian troops, with batteries of the Royal Artillery and a company of engineers, was under the command of Major-General Sir John Michel, K.C.B.

The 2nd Division, composed of the 3rd (Buffs), the 44th, the 67th, and the 99th (Lanarkshire) regiments, the 8th and 19th Punjaub infantry, with similar equipment of artillery and engineers, was under the command of Major-General Sir Robert Napier, K.C.B. The cavalry brigade was made up of the 1st Dragoon Guards, one of our crack regiments, and Probyn's and Fane's regiments of Irregular Native Cavalry, which, under their dashing leaders, had gained a great reputation during the mutiny.

The French force, sent direct from France, assembled at Shanghai. It was under the command of General de Montaubon, a typical *"beau sabreur*" of the army of the emperor.

Lieutenant-General Sir Hope Grant, of Indian fame, was in command of the whole expeditionary force.

The British and French commanders were at Shanghai when the reply to the joint ultimatum of the Allies was received by Mr. Bruce, the British representative there. It was, as Sir Hope himself expressed it, "cheeky in the extreme." The following extract of the official communication shows this clearly:—

> For the future the British minister must not be so wanting in decorum. It will behove him not to adhere obstinately to his own opinion, for by so doing he will give cause for much trouble hereafter.

It was decided on receipt of this extraordinary document, early in April, to commence operations at once. Towards the end of May all preparations for the campaign in the north were completed, and by the end of July the combined French and British fleets of warships and transports stood off the mouth of the Peiho River, and the troops were able to discern in the distance the boasted Taku Forts, at which a British admiral had been previously repulsed, and which it was their immediate objective to take by assault.

The forts were situated two on each bank of the Peiho, several miles distant from the mouth, the strongest being the larger one. They were built on the extremity of the firm ground, in front of them being a great expanse of deep and sticky mud, to land on which and to storm the forts would have been an impossibility. It was therefore decided to land at Pehtang, a town and forts standing on the river of that name to the north of the Peiho, and advance from this direction to the assault of the Taku Forts.

It was rumoured throughout the fleet that the Emperor of China had sent a message to General Grant, informing him that a picket of 40,000 Tartars was lying in wait at Pehtang Forts, "with a force of 200,000 under the commander-in-chief, Sang-ko-lin-sin, between that and Tientsin." He therefore recommended the general to go away, if he valued the lives of himself and his people.

The disembarkation of the troops at about 2,000 yards from the Pehtang Forts, on the afternoon of the 1st August, was accomplished.

During the night an officer penetrated into the town, and discovered it had been abandoned by the Chinese soldiers, and that most of the guns in the town were only wooden dummies.

At length, on the 12th August, the general advance commenced, ten thousand British and five thousand French participating. The first British division, with the French, moved along the causeway, to attack the Chinese entrenched position at Sinho, while the 2nd Division and the cavalry diverged to the right, to cut off the retreat of the enemy. The march of these latter troops was laborious in the extreme, the mud being knee-deep, but, after four miles, harder ground was reached, and the troops found themselves faced by an extended line of Tartar cavalry.

Our new Armstrong guns, then for the first time tested in actual warfare, began to create great havoc among the enemy, whose wretched *gingals* and small field guns were absolutely ineffective at the long range. For a time, however, the Tartars bore this destructive fire well, and finally succeeded in effecting a well-directed charge in spite of it. Our cavalry, however, speedily put them to the rout, and the exhausted state of our horses alone prevented a lengthy pursuit and a heavier loss to the enemy.

Meanwhile, on the causeway, the 1st Division was engaged in bombarding the enemy's entrenched position, and after twenty-five minutes the latter found their position untenable. Here, as elsewhere, our cavalry were too exhausted to pursue, and the field guns were hurried forward to pour their deadly volleys into the masses of retreating Tartars.

By the afternoon the Battle of Sinho was virtually over, though individual skirmishes still took place. Our loss was only two killed and some dozen wounded, and the French casualty list was equally light. The loss of the enemy, however, was very heavy, the plain being dotted with Tartar corpses for a long distance, while dead bodies in heaps lay within the enemy's entrenchments. Considering, however, that the Allied troops outnumbered the enemy by two to one, it must be admitted, with General Napier, that the enemy "had behaved with courageous endurance."

At the conclusion of the engagement at Sinho, it was discovered by the Allied commanders that the force there encountered was but a strong outpost, the main body of the enemy being located behind entrenchments at Tang-ku, some three miles further along the causeway.

Accordingly, Sir Hope Grant decided to postpone the forthcoming action until the morrow, the remainder of the day and night being spent in pushing forward our heavy guns up to the Chinese position and in digging pits for our riflemen. At half-past five in the morning the 1st Division pushed forward to storm the Chinese position, the 2nd Division being held in reserve. The contest was sharp and short, the Chinese replying with spirit to our fire, which from our 42 heavy guns was destructive in the extreme.

Some explanation of the tenacity with which they stood to their guns was afterwards forthcoming, when it was found that many of the wretched gunners had been tied to the pieces of ordnance which they served!

After the enemy's fire had been silenced, our infantry dashed forward, and the foremost of our men, the Rifles, found themselves just in time to bayonet some of the last of the Tartar defenders. The fugitives could be seen streaming out of the village towards a bridge of boats spanning the Peiho, by which they reached the village of Taku upon the further bank of the river. Though no precise estimate of the enemy's dead could be obtained, dozens of them lay amongst the guns, dozens more in the ditches, scores had been swept down the river in junks or borne off by comrades, and numbers had crawled down to the village to die. The full opposing force was estimated at 6,000. The Allies' casualties amounted to 15 wounded, not a man having been killed.

The way was now clear for an attack upon the Taku forts. Some disagreement arose as to which of the four should be the first object of the Allied attack. The French were in favour of first assaulting the larger southern fort, the strongest of the four, but Sir Hope Grant, observing that the nearer of the northern forts, though small, commanded all the others, decided, in spite of the French protest, to make this the object of attack. Several days were spent in preparation, road-making, and the like, and during the night of the 20th August, after a hard night's labour, everything was found to be in order for the attack.

Bridges had been thrown over the principal canals, intersecting the country, batteries had been erected near the forts, and twenty heavy guns and three mortars were mounted, four British and four French gunboats moved up the river to join in the attack, and a storming party of 2,500 British, consisting of a wing of the 44th, a wing of the 67th, and two detachments of marines, together with 1,000 French, mustered under Brigadier Reeves for what was to prove the hardest fight of the campaign.

At daybreak our batteries and gunboats opened fire, the fort replying briskly, and the engagement was begun. Hotter and hotter grew the cannonade, and after an hour had passed and our storming party

THE 67TH TAKING FORT TAKU

was in momentary expectation of receiving orders to advance, suddenly a tall black pillar of smoke was seen to shoot up from the fort in front, and immediately afterwards to burst at a great height like a rocket. The earth shook for many miles. A magazine had blown up.

The enemy's fire ceased for a moment, but the garrison seemed to be determined to serve their guns so long as one of them remained, and manfully reopened fire. Half an hour later a similar explosion occurred in the second northern fort, having apparently been caused by a stray shell from the gunboats. By seven o'clock, the large guns of the enemy having been silenced, and a small breach made in the wall, the storming party received orders to advance.

As the men went forward into the open, they were assailed by a hail of bullets by the Chinese, and many wounded began to drop in the line of advance. The British portion of the force was sadly hampered by the necessity of carrying sections of the pontoon bridge by which it was intended to span the two ditches which ran round the front of the fort.

After all their exertions, however, the bridge proved useless, a round shot in one instant completely smashing one section, and knocking over the fifteen men who carried it. The French, on the other hand, carried light bamboo ladders, which proved sufficiently effective to enable them to cross the ditch, whilst our men had to swim or struggle over as best they could.

The first ditch crossed, a formidable obstacle presented itself. The intervening twenty feet of ground between the ditches had been thickly planted with sharp-pointed bamboo stakes, over which it was almost impossible to walk. It was here that our greatest loss occurred. Missiles of all descriptions rained down upon our troops halted before this formidable obstruction. Arrows, handfuls of slugs, pots of lime, and round shot thrown by hand constituted the enemy's ammunition, and now and again the defenders leapt upon the walls to take more careful aim at the attacking force.

At length, a few men succeeded in reaching the walls, and while the French were fruitlessly endeavouring to plant their scaling ladders, Colonel Mann and Major Anson, perceiving the drawbridge tied up with rope, cut it free with their swords. The bridge fell with a crash, and was totally wrecked by its fall. Eventually, however, a long beam was thrown across, and one by one our men advanced across it to the walls. The progress was slow, a considerable number of the men being unable to perform this feat with success, and numbers of them fell into the muddy ditch below, among the hilarious laughter of their comrades, which even the near presence of death failed to damp.

By this time ladders had been dragged over by the French in considerable numbers, and planted here and there against the walls, only to be thrown back by the active defenders. The British meanwhile running round the walls, eagerly sought a scalable place.

At last, a French soldier holding aloft the tricolour, with a wild cheer on his lips, succeeded in placing his foot upon the parapet for a moment before falling back dead. His comrades were immediately in his place.

Almost simultaneously young Chaplin, an ensign of the 67th, holding high the Queen's colours of his regiment, half scrambled and was half pushed up the wall, and, amid the wild hurrahs of his men, planted his flag upon the parapet, where it fluttered in the breeze. A sharp conflict took place the instant after at the nearest battery upon the wall, and before the enemy were driven off young Chaplin received several severe wounds.

Already a number of British had penetrated through a small breach in the wall, and, entering the streets below, had come to a hand-to-hand encounter with the garrison. Headed by their stalwart commander, the Chinese with unwonted courage presented a bold front to our advancing troops, and for a moment a desperate struggle ensued. Then, as their leader, who proved to be the commander of the forces, fighting in the front rank, and refusing to submit, fell dead, they turned and fled pell-mell through the streets. Unhappily for them, the same obstructions which had so hampered the advance of our troops, now lay in their line of retreat, and as they endeavoured to struggle through the ditch and over the staked ground, a great slaughter look place.

Colonel Wolseley said:—

Never, did the interior of any place testify more plainly to the noble manner in which it had been defended. The garrison had evidently determined to fall beneath its ruins, or to the last had been so confident that they had never contemplated retreat. Probably the stoutness of the resistance was due to the example of the Chinese commander, an exceedingly rare one, it being proverbial among the Chinese that the officers are almost always the first to bolt when, defeat seems probable.

Preparations were immediately made for an advance on the second northern fort, when suddenly a white flag was hoisted on the principal fort on the southern bank, and a *mandarin* was rowed over in a boat to treat for terms. He could not, however, give any definite assurance of capitulation, and he was told that if the second fort was not surrendered in two hours it would be taken by storm.

The allotted time passed, and our men advanced to the attack. Not a shot was fired on them, nor any sign of resistance made, and suddenly, to the astonishment of all, down went the flags of the fort. The troops entered and found the garrison of 2,000 all huddled together in one place like so many sheep. It was a sudden transformation, since they had thrown away their arms and evidently expected nothing less than massacre, being much astonished when they were sent over to the other side in boats, and allowed to go where they pleased.

The Chinese were evidently completely cowed, and, after some of the usual shilly-shallying, the *mandarin* in command of the southern forts delivered them into our hands, "together with the unconditional surrender of the whole country on the banks of the Peiho, as far as Tientsin."

This struggle cost the British 67 men killed and 22 officers and 161 men wounded. The casualties of the French numbered 130. The Chinese dead lay everywhere, within and without the forts, and their loss must have exceeded 2,000 killed.

Thus, with the capture of the Taku forts, boasted as impregnable throughout the Chinese Empire, ended the first stage of the war. The gunboats cleared the way of the rows of iron stakes and ponderous booms which obstructed the passage of the river, and by the first week of September the Allied troops, with the exception of the Buffs, left to garrison Taku, and a wing of the 44th regiment sent to Shanghai, which was at that time threatened by the Taiping rebels, were in quarters at Tientsin.

For a time, it appeared that the war was ended. The Chinese Government professed great anxiety for peace, and Lord Elgin, our ambassador, who accompanied the troops, was in daily communication with its emissaries. Treachery, however, was feared, and the Chinese duplicity being well known, the advance on Pekin was decided on.

On the 8th September the 1st British Division and half the French force moved out of Tientsin, the remainder being left in the town owing to inadequate means of transport. When, on the 13th inst., the Allies reached the village of Hu-see-wu, it was arranged in response to the urgent entreaties of the Chinese that the army should halt within a mile and a half of the old walled city of Chang-dia-wan, and that

Lord Elgin, with 1,000 of an escort, should proceed to Tung-chow, to sign a convention with the Imperial Commissioners there, and then to proceed with the same escort to Pekin for its ratification.

Mr. Parkes, Lord Elgin's secretary, with some officers and an escort, set out in advance to arrange preliminaries, and while the main body were on their march upon the 18th, they were horrified, to hear the sounds of distant firing, and shortly afterwards a few of Mr. Parkes's party galloped up. They had had to fight their way through the Chinese, who had set upon them suddenly, and the remainder of the party had been captured.

Sir Hope Grant immediately prepared for battle. In front were at least 30,000 men, while the Allies numbered 3,500 in all, but there was no question of retreat. Seeing the Allies coming, the Chinese opened fire from skilfully-concealed batteries, which defended their five entrenched camps. For two hours the contest raged hotly, and, at the end of that time, the French troops on the left had carried the works in front of them, while Fane's Horse, dashing through the village street on their flanks, completed the enemy's rout. In the centre our artillery speedily silenced the enemy's guns, and the Tartar cavalry on the right were put to flight by the dragoons and Probyn's horse.

Our casualties did not amount to 40 in this engagement, while hundreds of the enemy were cut down by the cavalry in the long pursuit. Seventy-four pieces of cannon fell into our hands.

After halting for some days until the 2nd Division and the siege guns had come up, Sir Hope Grant on the 2nd October commenced the final march to Pekin. All overtures of peace were in the meantime rejected, until the captives should be delivered up to Lord Elgin. Progress through the dense country was slow, and numerous isolated skirmishes took place.

On the 7th October the French wing reached Yenn-ming-yenn, the famous summer palaces of the Emperors of China, and here a halt took place for several days, while the French gave themselves over to indiscriminate plunder and wanton destruction.

The army ran riot in the sacred precincts of the Imperial residences. Every French soldier had in his possession stores of gold watches, strings of pearls, and other treasures, while many of the officers amassed fortunes. The British, however, were prohibited from individual plundering, although a large number of the officers seized the opportunity of the halt to pay a visit to the palaces, and returned laden with booty.

So great was the amount of treasure brought back by these that when, on the instructions of Sir Hope Grant, the whole of the loot thus obtained was disposed of at a public auction which lasted over two days, and was certainly one of the most singular scenes ever witnessed, the share of each private soldier was not less than £4 sterling. Sir Hope Grant and his two generals of division renounced their own large shares of the booty, thereby sensibly increasing the gains of the private soldiery.

By the 12th of October the Allied Armies assembled before the Au-ting gate of Pekin, and demanded its surrender. On the 8th, Mr. Parkes and some of his party had been released, the Chinese alleging that these were all the prisoners they had in their possession; but we had reason to suppose that others remained in their hands. Accordingly, a battery was erected in front of the gate, and the enemy were given till noon to surrender the gate.

At five minutes to twelve General Napier stood watch in hand, and was about to give the order to fire when it was intimated that the gate had been surrendered. It was immediately taken possession of by our infantry, while the French marched with tricolours flying and drums beating. But though the gate was in our hands, the remaining prisoners had not yet been delivered up, and our guns were still pointing threateningly from the city gate, when in the afternoon eight Sikhs and some Frenchmen in an emaciated condition came into our camp.

On the 18th, the fate of the remaining prisoners was discovered, Colonel Wolseley coming on a cart containing coffins. These were opened, and from the clothing they were proved undoubtedly to be the missing men. It was found that they had been most cruelly done to death, and the rage of the troops at this discovery was near exceeding all bounds. Sir Hope, however, had given his word that the city should be spared, but as the Summer Palace had been the scene of these atrocities it was by Lord Elgin's orders razed to the ground. An indemnity of 100,000 was paid as compensation to the relatives of the murdered men.

Further preparations were made for a complete bombardment of Pekin, when, on the 24th October, peace was declared.

Chapter 9

The Battle of Arogee: 1868

The man who stands out most prominently in Abyssinian history is Theodore, the King of Kings of Ethiopia. He was a remarkable personage, perhaps the most remarkable who has appeared in Africa for some centuries. Having led the life of a lawless soldier, accustomed from childhood to witness the perpetration of the most barbarous acts of cruelty and oppression, there is only one standard by which to measure his career, and that an Abyssinian one.

The British Consul, Mr. Plowden, heard of his accession at Massowa, in March, 1855, and at one proceeded to join his camp, with the approval of the Foreign Office.

The news of Plowden's death having reached London, Captain Cameron was appointed to succeed him, it being the resolve of the Government to persevere in the policy of cultivating friendly relations with Abyssinia. The new consul was instructed to make Massowa his headquarters, and he was further directed to avoid becoming a partisan of any of the contending parties in the country. Cameron was well received by the king. He received a letter from Theodore, to be forwarded to the Queen of Britain. This strange epistle, which was received at the Foreign Office on February 12, 1863, contained a proposal to send an embassy to England, and a request that an answer might be forwarded through Consul Cameron.

On its arrival, the letter was put aside, and no answer was sent.

The letter, which was afterwards to become so famous, contained the following sentences:—

I hope Your Majesty is in good health. By the power of God, I am well. My fathers, the emperors, had forgotten our Creator. He handed over our kingdom to the Gallas and Turks. But God created me, lifted me out of the dust, and restored this empire to my rule.

Early in 1864, a young Irishman named Kerans, whom the consul had appointed as his secretary, arrived with despatches from Britain, which were seen by the king. Imagine the latter's wrath when there was no reply to his letter! Theodore felt insulted. Only one mode of retaliation could soothe his wounded feelings, and forthwith he adopted it. The British Consul and all his suite were put in prison. Cameron was afterwards tortured with ropes, and the whole party were sent to the fortress of Magdala and there put in irons.

Colonel Merryweather, our representative at Aden, after trying everything, despaired of securing the release of the prisoners by peaceful means. A warlike demonstration, he saw was inevitable, and in March, 1867, he reported to the home authorities that the last chance of effecting the liberation of the prisoners by conciliatory means had failed.

In July, 1867, the British Cabinet finally resolved to send an expedition to Abyssinia, to enforce the release of the captives.

Bombay having been fixed upon as the base of operations, the government of that Presidency was asked to make all the necessary arrangements. In August, Sir Robert Napier, the commander-in-chief of the Bombay Army, was appointed to command the expedition

The task which the force had to accomplish was to march over 400 miles of a mountainous and little-known region to the camp occupied by Theodore, and to use armed force to release the British officers whom he detained as prisoners.

The king had now broken up his camp at Debrataber. His power was entirely gone. His once great empire was wholly in the hands of rebels. Slowly towards his last stronghold he was marching, encumbered by his guns and mortars and by much heavy baggage. According to the campaign arranged, the British force and the king would advance on two lines which would meet at Magdala.

The army, under King Theodore, consisted of about 3,000 men, armed with percussion loaders, about 1,000 matchlock men, a mob of spearmen, and about 30 pieces of ordnance which his people could not properly handle. This rabble was to oppose the enormous disciplined Army of the British. Doubtless it was this fact which led Theodore to be described as being like "an exhausted, hunted lion, wearily seeking his lair, to die there unconquered and at bay."

When Sir Robert Napier arrived upon the scene of operations, upwards of 7,500 of his men were ready to give battle. Two courses were then open to him. He could have chosen to intercept Theodore in his flank march before he reached Magdala, and so prevent the prisoners falling completely into his power, or, by the alternative plan, which was adopted, allow Theodore to reach Magdala at his leisure, with all his guns, and thus place the British prisoners at his mercy.

The beginning of February saw the pioneer force under the General marching on the road from Adyerat to Antalo. The difficulties of the road were great, but the indomitable zeal and energy of the force overcame them. Along the route the force was well received by the people. The commander took care to leave a good impression behind him, and this he did in several ways, but especially by the prompt payment he ordered for everything that was brought for sale.

Theodore was also marching to Magdala, and he had surmounted difficulties in a manner that was afterwards to astonish his foes. He had odds against him, but he knew every inch of the country, and won the race. Still, the king had already sealed his own doom. He had devastated his one faithful province of Bagemder. He burned Gondar, destroyed all the villages round Debrataber, and put to death in the cruellest manner possible three thousand persons in the course of eighteen months. There could only be one result of such barbarism. The inhabitants of Bagemder, hitherto devoted to the king's person, rose against the tyrant and his diminishing army. Such a state of affairs could not last long. The king had reduced a rich province to a desert, and in order to keep his troops alive it was necessary that he should move.

Back fell the king upon his fortress, his last hope in this his time of bitter experience. He began his wonderful march in October, 1867. It was forlorn, but magnificent, and at once stamps Theodore as a man of brilliant resource. With no base of operations, surrounded on every side by enemies, and with the ever-present necessity of constructing roads over which to take his heavy artillery, he achieved what his own countrymen had described as an impossibility. By the 1st March, 1868, the king saw the end of his wonderful undertaking approach.

All that remained was to drag the heavy ordnance up the Warkwaha valley to Arogee, and thence up the steep declivity of the Fala saddle to Islamgye, at the foot of Magdala. The king now spoke frequently of the advance of the British. One day he remarked:—

With love and friendship, the English will conquer me, but if they come otherwise I know that they will not spare, and I shall make a bloodbath and die.

On the day Theodore's army arrived at Arogee, he sent orders up to Magdala that the irons were to be removed from Mr. Rassam. This might be taken as a sign that the king was about to relent, but it was too late—a fact which he seems to have realised himself very shortly after. His conduct now became eccentric in the extreme. He invited the British prisoners to come down to Islamgye and see the great mortar brought up. When the operation was completed, the king conversed with the prisoners, and said that if only his power had been as strong as it was a few years ago, he would have gone to meet the British on landing. Now, however, he had lost all Abyssinia, and had only that rock upon which he must needs wait for them.

Stranger than ever, this once mighty ruler of men admitted to Mr. Rassam that when he was excited, he was not responsible for his actions. This was soon proved. On one occasion when the king had drank to excess, he was aroused by the clamouring of the native prisoners he had released. Enraged at this, he ordered them all to be put to death, commencing the work of execution himself. Many were hurled alive over the precipice, and those who showed signs of life were shot down by the soldiers. The massacre lasted for three hours, and was responsible for two hundred deaths. According to one of his body-servants, Theodore spent most of the night, after this massacre, in prayer, and was heard to confess that he had been drunk when he committed it.

Meantime, on the 28th March, the British commander-in-chief had encamped at Santava. Two days later the 2nd Brigade arrived, accompanied by the naval brigade from the *Rocket*, under Captain Fellowes of the *Dryad*. As usual, the bluejackets were the very life of the force. They chummed with the native troops. They joked and laughed and danced, and kept everybody in good humour. The close friendship between the sailors and the Sikhs was most amusing. The latter could not speak a word of English, and yet the jolly tars seemed to understand their every wish.

The two hostile forces, which for months had been converging from Debratabor and the sea to the same point at Magdala, were now nearly face to face.

Markham says:—

On that dark basaltic rock, was the hunted fallen king, with only 3,000 soldiers, armed with percussion guns and matchlocks, a rabble of spearmen, and a number of pieces of ordnance which his strong will had created, but which hie people knew not how to use. Only a faithful few of his followers could be depended on to stand by their brave master to the bitter end. His mighty prestige alone kept the shattered remains of his army together.

So much for the predicament in which Theodore found himself. Now for the British position. In numbers they were nearly equal to the enemy. They were armed and provided with all that science could suggest for such an undertaking, besides, they were in a friendly country, and had abundant supplies.

Bitter must have been the fallen Theodore's reflections now. How he must have sighed for some of his lost power and might as he realised the magnitude of the task awaiting him! Yet he had some power left. The prisoners were still in his hands. It was quite possible for him to make the one object of his enemies turn out badly.

Early on 10th April the 1st Brigade, under Sir Charles Staveley, began the descent of the Beshilo Ravine. The brigade was led up the steep Gumbaji Spur towards Aficho. The 2nd Brigade, under the commander-in-chief, followed. The cavalry was ordered to remain at Beshilo, with instructions to be in readiness to advance when called upon. It was not intended that the fight should begin before dark.

Colonel Phayre had ascertained that Wark-waha valley was unoccupied by the enemy. A message to this effect was accordingly sent to Sir Robert Napier. Staveley, through whose hands the communication had passed, advanced along the heights, and Napier ordered the naval brigade, A battery, and the baggage to follow the king's road up the Wark-waha ravine. Napier and his staff rode up to the front in the course of the afternoon, and were present at the action. Meanwhile Colonel Phayre reconnoitred the country so far as Arogee plain, and the 1st Brigade advanced along the Aficho plateau.

Right in front loomed Theodore's stronghold, a thousand feet above. All was silence, and nothing stirred to break or mar the stillness. Time passed, and the British force waited anxiously. At last, the silence was broken! Between four and five in the afternoon a gun was fired from the crest of Talla, 1,200 feet above Arogee. It was followed by another and still another, until the air seemed full of the sound of musketry. Then the British soldiery were amazed and startled. The very pick of Theodore's army poured down upon them, yelling defiance as they came.

It was a trying moment, but the British bluejackets were not long in realising what it meant. In an instant they got their rocket tubes into position, and opened fire upon the enemy coming from the heights. Staveley also acted without loss of time. All the infantry of his brigade were moved down the steep descent to Arogee. Then the snider rifles opened a fire which no troops on earth could have withstood.

The Abyssinians were simply mowed down. Unable to get within range with their antiquated rifles, they became merely a target for the British fire. Hope must have left them then. Led on by the gallant old warrior, the Fitaurari-Gabriyi, they returned again and again to the charge with great bravery. But men could not struggle against machines. The most heroic courage that ever filled the hearts of heroes was without avail in face of such unequal odds. While the battle of Arogee was in progress, a thunderstorm broke over Magdala, and the roar of the thunder seemed to struggle for mastery against the roar of artillery.

Night came on and stopped the action. It was then found that Gabriyi and most of his chief officers were dead. Slowly the broken Abyssinian force made its way back to Magdala. There was no disorder, and now and then a cheer could be heard from the throats of the defeated warriors. A detachment of the enemy was still left, however, and it advanced to attack the British baggage train. Some stiff fighting followed, in which the gallantry of Theodore's followers was again manifest.

Driven back again and again with great slaughter, the Abyssinians continued to advance, heedless of all danger, until they were checked by the baggage guard. Those of the enemy who had got into the ravine were hemmed in, and their loss was terrible. The Dam-wanz that night is said to have been choked up with dead and dying men, and the little rill at the bottom of the ravine ran red with blood.

The main body of the enemy, too, had not yet reached safety. The bluejackets had taken up a position more to the front, and into the retreating force they sent rockets, with terrible effect. Shots were also fired at the crest of Talla, whence the guns of Theodore had played, but just when they had got the exact range the naval brigade were ordered to cease firing.

The Abyssinians estimated their force at 3,000 armed with guns and matchlocks, and about 1,000 spearmen. Of these, from 700 to 800 were killed—349 having been killed on the left attack alone; 1,500 were wounded, most of them severely. Many of the survivors fled without returning to Magdala, and all night the Abyssinians were calling to their wounded comrades, and carrying them off the field.

The British numbered close on 2,000 men, of whom Captain Roberts and six men of the 4th, twelve of the Punjaub Pioneers, and one Bombay sapper were wounded—two mortally, nine severely, and nine slightly. Four of the wounds inflicted on the Pioneers were from spears, which proved that the fighting was not all on the side of the British.

It was computed that 18,000 rounds of musketry were fired by the British. The action will be remembered in military history as the first in which the Snider rifle was used.

Touching in the extreme is the description of events in Theodore's camp on the night of the Arogee battle.

As the shades of evening closed round, Theodore looked down and saw his army reeling under the deadly fire of the British troops. He walked, sad and desponding, to the foot of the Selas-syé Peak, and there in the thick darkness, with peals of thunder resounding over his head, he waited for the return of his chiefs and soldiers. Then a broken remnant began to crowd about him, coming up the steep path. . . . At a glance he saw it all. His army was broken and destroyed, and no hope was left but in concession to an invincible enemy. At midnight he deputed Mr. Flad and Mr. Waldmeier to go up to Magdala and make proposals of peace to Mr. Rassam, confessing that with the destruction of his army his power was gone.

CHAPTER 10

The Storming of Magdala: 1868

After the day of slaughter at Arogee, Sir Robert Napier hesitated. The safety of the captives was ever in his mind. Upon his forbearance depended their lives, and the signal success of the campaign. A perceptible movement upon Magdala might have deprived the desperate Theodore of every ray of hope, and have caused him to order the immediate slaughter of the captives. And so, Sir Robert Napier decided to ask Theodore to surrender. His messengers were actually on their way to the emperor with a peremptory demand to this effect when they met two strangers, who turned out to belong to the band of captives. The whole party thereupon, returned to the British camp. On arrival, one of the captives who had been sent as a messenger by Theodore spoke to Sir Robert.

I have been sent down to you, Sir Robert, by the emperor, to ask why it is you have come to this country, what it is you want, and whether you will return to your own country if the captives are released?

Sir Robert's reply, which he asked the two messengers to convey to Theodore, was explicit in the extreme.

Tell him from me, that I require an instant surrender of the prisoners, with their property, of himself, with the fortresses of Selasse and Fahla, Magdala and all therein. He may rest assured that honourable treatment will be accorded him.

The captives fulfilled their mission. Theodore was furious, and again he sent them down to the British general with a petition for better terms, "as he was a king, and could not surrender himself to any chief who served a woman. Rather than surrender," he added, "I will fight to the death. Can you not be satisfied with the possession of those you came for, and leave me alone in peace?"

They were sent back by Napier with the message:—

You must surrender yourself unconditionally to the Queen of Britain. Be assured that honourable treatment will be accorded you.

It was then that Rassam, another of the captives, did a very diplomatic thing. He asked the king to repose his trust in him, let the captives go free to the camp, and he guaranteed that the British chief would return to his own country. The king believed in Rassam. He trusted to his influence to reconcile him with the commander-in-chief, and gave him orders to assemble immediately all the European captives, with their property, at the Thafurbate gate of the fortress.

The parting scene was a strange one. Theodore addressed each and all of the captives in an affectionate manner, wishing some of them well, and asking others to forgive him for what he had done to them. As soon as news of their release reached the army, the soldiers hurried to headquarters by hundreds to await their arrival, and eager crowds greeted them. Sixty-one in number, they looked to be in good condition, and were objects of great interest to all.

On Easter Sunday 1,000 beeves and 500 sheep were sent by Theodore to Sir Robert Napier, with the hope that the British soldiers would eat their fill and be merry. But Sir Robert was not to be caught napping. He sent an officer up to Magdala to say that he couldn't think of accepting anything from His Majesty until himself, his family, and his fortresses were surrendered to the Queen of Britain.

Meanwhile, preparations had been proceeding for taking Magdala by storm, Escalading ladders were made out of *dhoolie* poles; powder charges, hand grenades, etc. were also made ready for use. The elephants brought up the Armstrong battery to the camp, and, in short, everything was ready for a grand assault, which was expected to take place at noon the following day.

On the morning of Easter Monday, April 13, 1868, there arrived at the British camp eight Abyssinians, richly apparelled. One look sufficed to show that they were chiefs of high degree. Ushered into the presence of the commander-in-chief they stated that they came down to offer Fahla and Selasse on condition that they were allowed to depart unmolested. Their conditions were promptly accepted. They were then questioned as to the whereabouts of Theodore. Their answer was a profound surprise to the British general. They said they expected that the king had either gone to Gojam or to the camp of the Galla Queen Mastevat. Who would have dreamt that the king would have left his fortress? Still, the fact was apparently indisputable, and Napier promptly adopted means for the capture of the missing monarch.

He at once offered a reward of 50,000 dollars for Theodore, dead or alive, and messengers with this announcement were at once despatched to all the neighbouring camps. Next Sir Robert resolved to occupy Fahla and Selasse, and to move upon Magdala. Regiments in columns of fours proceeded to Fahla Plain. First came the Duke of Wellington's Own—a regiment destined to play an important part in the forthcoming last act of the Abyssinian campaign. The road was steep and difficult to negotiate, but the troops, in toiling on, passed enormous boulders until they found themselves full under the noon-day sun, on the crest of the gorge between Fahla and Selasse.

On arrival at the heights, six companies of the 33rd Foot advanced with bayonets fixed, driving the natives before them out of the fortress. The chiefs were assured that their people would not be harmed, but that they must leave at once for the plain. As the natives emerged from the pass they were disarmed. When they reached the terraced ridge, where the army was halted, they drew back in fear, but they were soon reassured. Men, women and children were eager to greet the soldiers, for the chiefs had assured them that these were their best friends.

While this strange scene was being witnessed, Colonel Loch and Captain Speedy were manoeuvring at the extremity of Selasse, on the road which encircled the fortress and thence led to Magdala. Looking up to the heights the British officers saw a number of men careering about on the plateau which connected Selasse with Magdala. It was ascertained that they belonged to the enemy, and their dress indicated that they were chiefs. When these men saw the cavalry advancing round the corner at Selasse they retired slowly and in good order to Magdala, firing as they went.

As the British proceeded, the officers soon discovered the meaning of the presence of the Abyssinians. They had been attempting to secure a number of cannon and mortars lying at the Selasse end of the plateau. The cannon were at once seized by our men, and were found to be mostly of French and British manufacture.

After retiring as far as the foot of Magdala, a few of the Abyssinians made a pretence of preparing to charge, but apparently hesitated. Along the brow of the famous fortress many dark heads could be seen, and now and then shots awoke the echoes. Suddenly the Abyssinians who were first noticed made a dash towards Captain Speedy and the artillery, which accompanied him. After coming within three hundred yards the natives halted, and judge of the surprise of the British officers when they discovered that the foremost among the company of horsemen was no other than Theodore, king of Abyssinia

Such a discovery was of course highly satisfactory to the British, who had been somewhat downcast at the report of the king's escape.

As showing the reckless courage of the king, it is said that his words of greeting to the British were, "Come on! Are ye women, that ye hesitate to attack a few warriors?"

As Theodore and his followers showed a disposition to advance, some soldiers of the 33rd were ordered to take up a position commanding all paths leading to the valleys on all sides of the plateau. A company of the 33rd, who had eagerly ascended Selasse for the purpose of planting their colours on its rampart, were also invited to aid in the defence of the captured artillery.

A few shells were now sent whizzing amongst the Abyssinians, who had by this time commenced a desultory firing. Very soon, growing alarmed at the work of our artillery, the Abyssinians retired for shelter behind some wooden booths. A few more shells, however, soon dislodged Theodore and his men from their hiding places, and they beat a rapid retreat towards Magdala. Still they had not finished, and continued to fire at all who came within reach of their mountain stronghold. Their persistent firing ultimately lured a detachment of the 33rd Foot into action, but without marked effect, and shortly after this, orders came from Sir Charles Staveley to cease firing. At the same time the British flag was hoisted above Selasse and Fahla. Only Magdala now remained.

Describing the stronghold, one of the correspondents present says:—

Suppose a platform of rock, oval in shape, and a mile and a half in length, and from a half to three-quarters of a mile in width, rising five hundred feet perpendicularly about a narrow plateau, which connected its northern end with Selasse. The rock was Magdala, the plateau Islamgee. On the western and southern sides Magdala towered above the valley of the Melkaschillo some two thousand feet. The eastern side rose in three terraces of about 600 feet in height, one above another. Its whole summit was covered with house's, straw-thatched, and of a conical shape. The extreme brow of the fortress was defended by a stone wall, on the top of which a hurdle revetment was planted. But the side fronting Islamgee was defended by a lower wall and revetment constructed nearly half way up the slope. In the centre of the revetment was a barbican, up to which led the only available road to the fortress.

Fahla and Selasse having been left in the hands of sufficient garrisons, the remainder of the British troops were withdrawn to Islamgee, where they were halted behind the captured artillery. Sir Robert Napier had been at great pains to ascertain the strength of the fortress. One thing he had made sure of, that at only one point was it assailable, and that was the side which fronted the troops as they stood upon Islamgee.

Then Napier distributed his force in preparation for the attack. Soon twenty guns were thundering at the gates. Theodore could not misunderstand the meaning of the British now. It was surrender or death for him and his followers.

The bombardment lasted two hours. At the end of this period Napier had made up his mind that the defenders were weak, and that the British troops would suffer very little loss in the assault. He therefore ordered the Royal Engineers, the 33rd, the 45th, and the King's Own to be prepared to carry on the attack. Already the fire from the fortress had ceased. Soon signals for rapid firing were given to the British artillery, and under the furious cannonade which proceeded, the British troops began their march along the plateau.

Upon their arrival within fifty yards of the foot of Magdala, the order was given to the artillery to cease fire. Then the Engineers at once brought their sniders into play, and for ten minutes they and the 33rd and 45th rained a storm of leaden pellets upon the defenders.

Theodore and his brave followers had been concealed while the artillery was at work. Now, however, the king showed himself. Up he sprang, singing out his war-cry, and with his bodyguard he hastened to the gates, prepared to give the invaders a fitting welcome. He posted his men at the loopholes and along the wall, topped with wattled hurdles. Soon his signal was given, and heavy firing was directed upon the advancing soldiers, several of whom were wounded.

Next the British fire was concentrated on the barbican and the revetment, through the loopholes of which rays of smoke issuing forth betrayed the presence of the enemy. Slowly the soldiers advanced through the rain which accompanied the thunderstorm which now raged. For a minute there was a pause, and then again, a dozen bullets hurtled through the advance guard of the troops, wounding Major Pritchard and several of the Engineers. Then Major Pritchard and Lieutenant Morgan made a dash upon the barbican. They found the gate closed, and the inside of the square completely blocked up with huge stones.

A drummer of the 33rd climbed up the cliff wall. Reaching a ledge, he ascended another, and shouted to his companions to "Come on!" as he had found a way. In a short time, the intrepid soldiers had passed all the lower defences, and scattering themselves over the ground they made a rush for the other defence, 75 feet above them, passing over not a few ghastly reminders of the battle. There were obstacles in the way, but they could not stop the excited Irishmen. They leaped forward and fired volley after volley into the faces of the Abyssinians.

Nor must we forget the charge of Drummer Maguire and Private Bergin upon Magdala. It is related that the two men were advancing a few paces from each other to the upper revetment when they saw about a dozen of the enemy aiming at them. The doughty pair immediately opened fire, and so quick and well-directed was it that but few of their assailants escaped. Seeing a host of red-coats advancing upward, the others retreated precipitately. Over the upper revetment both men made their way, and at the same time they observed a man standing near a grass stack with a revolver in his hand.

When he saw them prepare to fire, he ran behind it, and both men plainly heard the shot fired which followed. Advancing, they found him prostrate on the ground, in a dying state, the revolver clutched convulsively in his right hand. To their minds the revolver was but their proper loot, and, without any ceremony, they wrenched it from the grasp of the dying man. The silver plate on the stock, however, arrested their attention, and, on examining it, they deciphered the following inscription:—

Presented by Victoria, Queen of Great Britain and Ireland, to Theodore, Emperor of Abyssinia, as a slight token of her gratitude for his kindness to her servant Plowden, 1854.

The soldiers were in the presence of the emperor, and he was dying. Soon the rest of the troops followed their leaders, and the British flag was straining from the post which crowned the summit of the Abyssinian stronghold. Then, while the sound of "God Save the Queen "rent the once more peaceful air, and the soldiers of the queen joined lustily in the triumphant cheers, the once proud Emperor of Abyssinia, in all the gorgeous trappings of his state, and surrounded by a crowd of interested spectators, breathed his last in the stronghold where he had thought to give pause to those he regarded as the enemies of his kingdom.

Soon after "the Advance" was once more sounded, and the soldiers filed in column through the narrow streets, the commander-in-chief and staff following.

When the cost of the assault came to be reckoned, it was found that 17 British had been wounded, though none of them mortally. The Abyssinian dead were estimated at 60, with double that number of wounded.

On the fourth morning after the fall of Magdala, the Abyssinians, to the number of 30,000, commenced their march for Dalanta. Every living soul having left, the gates were blown up, and the houses set on fire. The flames soon did their work, and nothing escaped.

On the 18th April, 1868, the troops turned their faces northward for their homeward march, their object fully attained.

CHAPTER 11

The Battles of Amoaful and Ordashu: 1874

For years the Ashantees had been a source of trouble and annoyance to the British settlers on the Gold Coast, and the campaign of 1873-74 was by no means entered upon without considerable provocation from this barbarous and fanatical people.

With the march of time, Britain, extended and strengthened her hold upon the settlement, and ultimately, pursuing this policy, brought out the Danes, and made exchanges with the Dutch there. These proceedings culminated in Britain becoming possessors of the whole of the territory formerly under Dutch protection. The taking over of the Dutch forts caused heart-burning among the Ashantees. Particularly was this the case with regard to Elimina, where, at the time the negotiations for the transfer were being considered, a number of Ashantee troops were lying.

King Koffee Kalkali, the ruler of the Ashantees, protested against the transfer, maintaining that the Dutch had no right to hand over the territory to Britain, as it belonged to him. Notwithstanding, the Dutch contrived to get rid of the truculent Koffee and his followers then stationed at Elimina.

Not only did the Ashantees resent the Anglo-Dutch agreement, but other tribes in several instances also took objection. This especially was the case as regarded the Fanties and Eliminas, who hated each other, and interchanged hostile acts, although by this time both were under one common protection.

The old hatred of Britain had been awakened. King Koffee assumed a dominant and aggressive spirit, and became bent on invasion. To some extent he was abetted by the Eliminas, who, in part at any rate, were disloyal to the whites. From these causes arose the campaign of '73-'74 and the Battles of Amoaful and Ordashu.

At the outbreak of hostilities, the British force available to resist attack was ridiculously meagre, numbering, it is computed, not more than. 600 men, scattered over several stations.

At home, the government was slow to act, and not until repeated application had been made for white troops was the appeal given heed to.

That renowned soldier Sir Garnet Wolseley was commissioned to operate against the Ashantees. The announcement gave great satisfaction. If the spirit of the wild tribe was to be crushed, it was felt that Sir Garnet was the man to do it. But his task was no light one, and without white troops the issue was doubly doubtful.

His instructions, briefly, were to drive the Ashantees back over the Prah, then to follow and punish them until they should consent to be peaceful, should release their prisoners, and comply with terms necessary to our own interests and those of humanity.

The deadly nature of the Coast, "the white man's grave," was doubtless a potent factor with the government in that they did not immediately acquiesce with Sir Garnet's request for white troops. But, as we know, the government at last acceded, and the regiments selected for service in that disease-pregnated country have added lustre to their fame and also another page of glorious history to the story of the pluck and endurance of Britain's soldiers.

The total number of troops under the command of Sir Garnet Wolseley being made up of Colonel Wood's native regiment of 400 men, Major Russell's native regiment of 400, the 42nd Highlanders (Black Watch) 575 strong, the Rifle Brigade 650, 75 men of the 23rd Fusiliers, Royal Naval Brigade 225, 2nd West India Regiment 350, Royal Engineers 40, and Rait's artillery 50.

About the end of October, 1873, Sir Garnet Wolseley began his forward march into the interior. There was fighting to be done ere long, for the enemy made an attempt to arrest the progress of the troops by besieging Abrakrampa, the chief town of the province of Abra, of which the native king was Britain's staunch, ally. A three days' ineffectual leaguer ensued, during which the Ashantees lost heavily, while not so much as one white man was injured. With Sir Garnet close behind, the Ashantees thought it best, to recross the Prah and retreat towards Coomassie.

Through the dense bush the troops marched in the garish and dazzling sunlight, and at the end of their daily tramp through the hostile country they were glad to lie down and rest in the huts provided for them. In the way of rations, the men were well looked after by the commissariat department, the fare being as follows:—One and a half pounds of meat, salt or fresh, one pound of pressed meat, one and a quarter pounds of biscuits, four ounces of pressed vegetables, two ounces of rice or preserved peas, three ounces of sugar, three-quarters of an ounce of tea, half an ounce of salt, one-thirteenth of an ounce of pepper. With such substantial and varied feeding the hardships of the march were minimised and weakness was rare—another striking illustration of the truth of the maxim of the great Napoleon that "an army goes upon its belly."

The further the British force progressed, denser and loftier grew the forest, although the Engineers with unflagging energy had cleared a pathway as far as the Prah. On the 15th December, 1873, Sir Garnet Wolseley was able to report:—

> The first phase of the war had been brought to a satisfactory conclusion by a few companies of the 2nd West India regiment, Rait's artillery, Gordon's Houssas, and Wood's and Russell's regiments, admirably conducted by the British officers belonging to them, without the assistance of any other troops except the marines and bluejackets who were upon the station on his arrival.

Sir Garnet arrived at Prashu on the 2nd January, 1874, and was joyfully received by the assembled soldiers. Early in the same morning an Ashantee embassy was espied on the other side of the Prah. These ambassadors brought a letter from the truculent King Koffee, in which the wily savage had the audacity to point out that the attack upon him was unjustifiable.

The *Times* correspondent wrote that:—

> Many stories were afloat about the King of Ashantee's proceedings. The following is a fair specimen, and illustrates well the extreme superstition of the Ashantees, showing by what influences Koffee is popularly supposed to be guided, and upon what councillors he is supposed to rely in the present crisis. Koffee, the story goes, recently summoned a great meeting of his fetish men, and sought their advice as to how he should act towards Britain, and whether he ought to seek for peace or stake his fortunes on the result of a war. The fetish men at first declined to give an answer, until they had been guaranteed that, no matter what their reply was, their lives should not be forfeited.
> Having been assured upon this point, they then replied that

'they saw everything dark, except the streets of Coomassie, which rail with blood.' King Koffee was dissatisfied with the vagueness of this reply, and determined to appeal still further to the oracle. He resorted to what he considered a final and conclusive test. Two he-goats were selected, one entirely black, the other of a spotless white colour, and, after due fetish ceremonies had been performed over the two goats, they were set at each other. The white goat easily overcame and killed his opponent. King Koffee, after this test, was satisfied that he was doomed to defeat at the hands of the white men.

He immediately sent the embassies before referred to, to seek for peace, but the object which was of greatest importance to him was to avoid the humiliation of seeing his territory invaded by the whites. When, however, he found that all his conciliatory overtures were powerless to hinder the advance of the British, the national pride of the chiefs and the ardour of the fighting population was too strong to admit of any restraint. These causes, combined with the threatened humiliation of seeing his capital invaded by the British and his fetish supremacy destroyed, nerved him for one desperate effort.

For this final move Sir Garnet was prepared. In his notes for the use of his army the commander says:—

Each soldier must remember that with his breech-loader he is equal to at least twenty Ashantees, wretchedly armed, as they are, with old flint muskets, firing slugs or pieces of stone that do not hurt badly at more than forty or fifty yards range. Our enemies have neither guns nor rockets, and have a superstitious dread of those used by us.

With these and similar heartening instructions, the coming fight was anticipated eagerly by our troops, the Fanties alone, who were employed as transport bearers, proving unreliable. These latter deserted in thousands, thus throwing extra work upon the white troops, many of the regiments having to carry their own baggage.

Information was received at the British headquarters on the 30th January, 1874, that a big battle was pending on the morrow. The natives were assembled in enormous strength, and were prepared to offer a stout resistance. On the eve of the fray the advance guard of the British force was at Quarman, a distance of not more than a couple of miles from Amoaful, one of the principal villages of the country. Between these two places lay the hamlet of Egginassie, and to this point Major Home's Engineers were busily engaged preparing a way for the advancing force.

In front of Amoaful 20,000 of the natives had taken up a position. Of this fanatical horde there was not a man but would be ready to perpetrate the most wanton cruelty, and to whom butchery was but second nature. As usual, the Ashantees were armed with muskets that fired slugs. They held a position of considerable strength upon the slopes of the hill that led to Amoaful. The dense nature of the bush, high walls of foliage, through which our troops had to pass, made it difficult for the soldiers to fire with precision, or make rapid progress.

The protection of not only our flanks, but also our rear, was a matter of special importance and anxiety, for in the enclosing screen of underwood it would be no difficult task for a stealthy and numerous foe to surround and decimate small detachments of the not over strong British force. But every precaution was taken to guard against surprise, and the British general had every confidence in each member of his force, officers and men alike.

The troops were early on the move, and with precision they filed into their allotted places. Led by Brigadier Sir Archibald Alison, the front column was comprised of the famous Black Watch, eighty men of the 23rd Fusiliers, Rait's artillery, two small rifled guns manned by Houssas, and two rocket troughs, with a detachment of the Royal Engineers. The left column was under the command of Brigadier McLeod, of the Black Watch, and contained half of the bluejackets, Russell's native troops, two rocket troughs, and Royal Engineers. Lieutenant-Colonel Wood, V.C., of the Perthshire Light Infantry, had charge of the right column, which consisted of the remaining half of the Naval Brigade, seamen and marines, detachments of the Royal Engineers, and artillery, with rockets and a regiment of African levies. The rear column was made up of the second battalion of the Rifle Brigade, 580 strong, and the entire force was under the skilful command of Sir Garnet Wolseley.

The forces were disposed so as to form a large square. By this means Sir Garnet hoped to nullify the favourite flank tactics of the enemy, but to some extent the formation had to be broken on account of the entangling brushwood.

The Battle of Amoaful was fought on the 31st January. Lord Gifford and his scouts were the first to get in touch with the enemy, and the desultory firing heard warned the leading column that the conflict was opening. The British forces met opposition about eight in the morning, and soon after the spirting of red musketry and the curl of white smoke were conspicuous in the dark, thick bush.

So fierce was the onslaught that it is calculated that had the Ashantees used bullets instead of slugs scarcely a man of the Black Watch would have lived to tell the tale. Nine officers and about a hundred men of the regiment were rendered useless by the blinding fire of the Ashantees. The marshy nature of the ground impeded progress, and in the underwood the skulking natives fired incessantly at the advancing troops.

Under a heavy fire, the left column were struggling to oust the enemy. There, while urging on his men, the gallant Captain Buckle, R.E., was mortally wounded, having been hit by two slugs in the region of the heart.

The troops succeeded in occupying the crest of the hill, where a clearing had been made, and the enemy was driven away from this position by an advance of the naval brigade and Russell's regiment.

Sir Garnet Wolseley says:—

Colonel McLeod, having cleared his front, and having lost touch of the left column, now cut his way in a north-easterly direction, and came into the rear of the Highlanders about the same hour that the advance occupied Amoaful. I protected his left rear by a detachment of the Rifle Brigade. Our left flank was now apparently clear of the enemy.

The right column were also soon hotly engaged, and so dense was the jungle between it and the main road that the men, in firing, had the greatest difficulty to avoid hitting their comrades of the Black Watch.

Mr. Henty, regarding this, says:—

Anxious to see the nature of the difficulties with which the troops were contending, I went out to the right column, and found the naval brigade lying down and firing into a dense bush, from which, in spite of their heavy firing, answering discharges came incessantly, at a distance of some twenty yards or so. The air above was literally alive with slugs, and a perfect shower of leaves continued to fall upon the earth. The sailors complained that either the 23rd or 42nd were firing at them, and the same complaint was made against the naval brigade by the 42nd and 23rd. No doubt there was, at times, justice in these complaints, for the bush was so bewilderingly dense that men soon lost all idea of the points of the compass, and fired in any direction from which shots came.

Casualties in the right columns were also numerous, and Colonel Wood, the commander, was brought in with an iron slug in his chest. The command of the wing now devolved on Captain Luxmore. But though the village was entered, the fighting was by no means at an end, and a final great effort was made by the Ashantees to turn the rear and drive the British from Amoaful. Sir Garnet immediately ordered the Rifle Brigade, hitherto unemployed in the battle, to take the back track and defend the line of communication towards Querman.

This was about one o'clock in the afternoon, and the Rifles succeeded in repulsing the natives. It will thus be seen that on all sides of the square the Ashantees had tried to break through. For more than an hour they maintained the attack, but the resistance offered completely set their attempts at nought. The climax came when Sir Garnet, observing that the Ashantee fire was slackening, gave orders for the line to advance, and to wheel round, so as to drive the enemy northwards before it.

The movement was splendidly carried out. The wild Kosses and Bonnymen of Wood's regiment, cannibals, who had fought steadily and silently so long as they had been on the defensive, now raised their shrill war-cry, slung their rifles, drew their cutlasses, and like so many wild beasts, dashed into the bush to close with the enemy, while the Rifles, quietly and in an orderly manner as if upon parade, went on in extended order, scouring every bush with their bullets, and in five minutes from the time the "Advance" sounded, the Ashantees were in full and final retreat. Even then the enemy were not inclined to take their beating without protest, and for several hours continued to harass the troops by sudden but abortive rushes.

Terrible carnage had been wrought on the Ashantees. The losses they suffered have been estimated at between 800 and 1,200 killed and wounded. The King of Mampon, who commanded the Ashantee right, was mortally wounded. Amanquatia, who commanded the left, was killed; and Appia, one of the great chiefs engaged in the centre, was also slain.

The British loss was over 200 officers and men killed and wounded, the Black Watch suffering most heavily, having one officer killed, and 7 officers and 104 men wounded. In his despatch Sir Garnet said:—

Nothing could have exceeded the admirable conduct of the

42nd Highlanders, on whom fell the hardest share of the work.

The highest praise for which any regiment could wish.

Having thus delivered a crushing blow to native power, the troops marched forward to complete the work which they had so well begun. It was evident that before the spirit of the Ashantee savage could be thoroughly broken Coomassie must be entered. Towards this end, Sir Garnet and his troops immediately set their faces.

Hard fighting, however, was not yet at an end, and on the day following the rout at Amoaful, February 1st, the Ashantees made a stand at Becquah, an important town standing a short distance from the line of communication, and which would undoubtedly have been the cause of considerable trouble and loss of life had the general moved directly north without causing the place to be destroyed.

Only about a mile separated the camp from Becquah, and the force creeping silently upon the village, soon engaged with the enemy. Sharp firing took place, and the natives, unable to withstand the assault, turned tail and fled. The men of the naval brigade were the first to enter the place, and soon the huts were a mass of flames. Some native accoutrements and much corn fell into our hands. Following this, several villages which lay between Amoaful and Coomassie were taken with comparatively little fighting, the Ashantees having evidently taken much to heart the severe loss inflicted on them on 31st January. Each village passed through had its human sacrifice lying in the middle of the path, for the purpose of affrighting the conquerors.

Mr. Stanley says:—

The sacrifice was of either sex, sometimes a young man, sometimes a woman. The head, severed from the body, was turned to meet the advancing army, the body was evenly laid out, with the feet towards Coomassie. This laying out meant no doubt, 'regard this fare, white men; ye whose feet are hurrying on to our capital, and learn the fate awaiting you.'

The spectacle was sickening, and the wanton cruelty made the victorious troops even more determined and anxious to put an end to these frightful barbarities.

From behind a series of ambuscades, the advance was again resisted at the River Ordah. After clearing out the enemy, it was learned that a large force had assembled at Ordashu, a village situated about a mile and a half beyond the northern bank of the river. Things had become serious for the Ashantees, and King Koffee now sent another letter to

Sir Garnet, imploring him to halt in order that he might gather the indemnity, at the same time promising to give up his hostages, the heir-apparent and the queen mother. Sir Garnet's reply was firm. He would march to Coomassie unless King Koffee fulfilled his promise by the next morning. The hostages failed to arrive, and the British troops were on the forward move at half-past seven in the morning.

The advance guard, consisting of Gifford's scouts, the Rifle Brigade, Russell's regiment, and Rait's artillery, were early in touch with the enemy, who had sought to impede progress at Ordashu. King Koffee himself directed the battle from a village nearly a couple of miles from the scene of conflict. As the successive companies marched up, they became engaged, and the firing was fast and furious. The enemy must now drive back the invaders or submit, and the throes of this final struggle for supremacy between barbarity and civilisation, the Ashantees fought with great bravery. But the Rifle Brigade proved as steady as a rock. When they moved it was forward, the rapid fire of the sniders and the well-placed shots of Rait's artillery gradually demoralising the defenders.

In this fashion the Rifle Brigade were gradually drawing close up to the village, and at the critical moment, with a ringing cheer and a rush, they carried the day. Although the village had been occupied the natives continued to rush to their doom, and the terrible loss inflicted on them by the Rifles was greatly added to by the naval brigade's fire and that of the troops of the main column, as they attempted to carry out their favourite flank movement.

The corpses lay thick on the roadside, while the bush was littered with dead and dying. Sir Garnet rushed the whole of the army through Ordashu, and then, without loss of time, "the Forty-Twa" were again in the van, heading towards Coomassie, a sufficient force having been left to guard Ordashu.

At Coomassie the troops had little difficulty in effecting occupation. The king and his household had fled, and further fight in the Ashantees there was none. Lord Gifford's scouts were the first to enter the town, and were followed by the Black Watch.

Coomassie, a veritable Golgotha, was razed to the ground, the palace destroyed, and the fierce spirit of the Ashantees quelled.

Chapter 12

The Battles with the Zulus: 1879

Says a writer in *Blackwood's Magazine*, in March, 1879:—

> To break the military power of the Zulu nation, to save our
> colonies from apprehensions which have been paralysing all
> efforts at advancement, and to transform the Zulus from the
> slaves of a despot who has shown himself both tyrannical and
> cruel, and as reckless of the lives as of the rights of his subjects
> ... is the task which has devolved upon us in South Africa, and
> to perform which our troops have crossed the Tugela.

Such causes enumerated above would appear to the unprejudiced
observer to be more than sufficient *raison d'être* for the British invasion of Zululand, but when one takes into account the unimpeachable
statements of those long resident in the adjacent colony of Natal, one
cannot help believing them to be a direct, if not wilful, misrepresenta-
tion of the facts.

The kingdom of Zululand in 1873 lay, as all are aware, between the
British colony of Natal on the south and the Transvaal Republic on the
north. Now, while the Natal border had always been in a state of quiet
and peacefulness, and the nearer settlers were on friendly terms with
their Zulu neighbours, the northern border of the kingdom was in a
constant state of unrest. For one thing, the Transvaal Boers were, upon
one pretext and another, constantly encroaching in a southerly direction on the confines of Zululand; for another, they were in the habit
of treating the Zulus and other tribes with an unpardonable severity.

The accusations brought above against Cetewayo, King of Zululand, appear also to have been largely unfounded. He was crowned,
at his own request, by the British Commissioner, on the 8th August,
1873, and had ruled his people well and in a fairly enlightened manner, though it is true he observed many barbarous native customs in

the punishment of Zulu offenders. He may, however, be declared to be a competent and capable native ruler.

Zululand being at this time under British protection, though ruled by Cetewayo, the Zulus were not permitted to resent the intrusions of the Boers upon their borders by a recourse to arms. When, however, on April 17, 1877, Great Britain, in the person of Sir Theophilus Shepstone, annexed the Transvaal Republic, on the ground of its mismanagement, incapability, and gross ill-treatment of the native races by slavery and other means, it was felt by Cetewayo that the time had at last come when the question of his disturbed border would be satisfactorily adjusted.

The Transvaal Boers were "paralysed" when the edict of annexation was read to them, and strong protests were issued to the British Government against this high-handed proceeding. Accordingly, every effort was made to conciliate the Boers until such time as they should have settled down under the new regime, almost the first of these concessions taking the form of an anti-Zulu view of the border question. Upon this question of the Transvaal-Zulu border, the whole matter of the war now turned.

As late as 1876 the Zulu people begged that:—

The Governor of Natal will take a strip of the country, the length and breadth of which is to be agreed upon between the Zulus and the commissioners (for whom they ask) sent from Natal, the strip to abut on the colony of Natal and to run to the northward and eastward in such a manner as to interpose all its length between the Boers and the Zulus, and to be governed by the colony of Natal.

Such a Commission was appointed, and, on December 11th, 1878, the boundary award was delivered to the Zulus at the Lower Tugela Drift. It was, on the whole, favourable to the Zulus, but so fenced about with warnings and restrictions as to be virtually negative in tone, and, in fact, many have asserted that by this time the British Government had made up its mind to the annexation of Zululand. In any event, the award was followed up with an ultimatum from Sir Bartle Frere, containing thirteen specific demands. One of these entailed the "disbanding of the Zulu Army, and the discontinuance of the Zulu military system."

By this time a considerable British force was present in Natal to protect the interests of the colony, and as a "means of defending whatever the British Government finds to be its unquestionable rights."

The reasons given for the issue of the ultimatum were three in particular. The first had reference to the affair of Sihayo. On July 28, 1878, a wife of the chief Sihayo, an under-chief of Cetewayo's, had left her husband and escaped into Natal. Hither she was followed by Sihayo's two chief sons and brother, conveyed back to Zululand, and there put to death in accordance with the native custom for such an offence. These culprits the Natal Government now demanded should be given up to be tried in the Natal courts. Cetewayo, however, did not regard the offence as a serious one, and offered money compensation in place of the surrender of the young men, "looking upon the whole affair as the act of rash boys, who, in their zeal for their father's honour, did not think what they were doing."

The demand for the person of the Swazi chief, Umbilini, formed the second point. This chief, a Swazi, was not under the jurisdiction of Cetewayo, and though he was charged, and had been frequently convicted of raiding, Cetewayo was in no way responsible for his acts, otherwise than as an overlord.

The temporary detention of two Englishmen, Messrs. Smith and Deighton, formed the third especial grievance, and for these several offences large fines in the way of cattle were demanded in the ultimatum. Says Miss Colenso, daughter of the then Bishop of Natal, and historian of the war:—

> The High Commissioner (Sir Bartle Frere) was plainly determined not to allow the Zulus the slightest 'law,' which, indeed, was wise in the interests of war, as there was considerable fear that, in spite of all grievances and vexations, Cetewayo, knowing full well, as he certainly did, that collision with the British must eventually result in his destruction, might prefer half a loaf to no bread, and submit to our exactions with what grace he could. And so probably he would; for from all accounts every effort was made by the king to collect the fines of cattle and propitiate the government.

Such efforts were, however, unavailing, owing to the shortness of time allowed for collecting the cattle, and no extension of the period was granted. Moreover, in the natural agitation caused among the Zulus by the grave turn events were taking, any concentration of troops on the other side of the border was construed into an intention on the part of the Zulu king to attack Natal, and urged as an additional reason for our beginning hostilities.

On the 11th January, 1879, the allotted period having expired, war was declared.

The document ran:—

The British forces are crossing into Zululand to exact from Cetewayo reparation for violations of British territory committed by the sons of Sihayo and others. (and to enforce better government of his people.) All who lay down their arms will be provided for, . . . and when the war is finished the British Government will make the best arrangements in its power for the future good government of the Zulus.

On the 4th inst., Lieutenant-General Lord Chelmsford, who had been resident in the colony since August, '78, was appointed commander-in-chief of Her Majesty's forces in South Africa,

Ulundi was to be the objective of the campaign, the British force to be divided into four columns, which should enter Zululand at four different points, and concentrated on Ulundi.

No. 1 Column, under Colonel Pearson, was to assemble on the Lower Tugela at Fort Pearson. It consisted of a company of the Royal Engineers, 2nd Battalion of the Buffs, 99th regiment, naval brigade with two guns and one gatling, one squadron of mounted infantry, about 200 Natal volunteers, two battalions of the 2nd regiment Natal native contingent, one company of Natal native pioneers, and a detachment of Royal Artillery.

No. 2 Column was to co-operate with No. 1. Colonel Dumford was in command, and the corps was composed almost entirely of natives; the Natal native horse, 315 in number, the Natal native contingent and pioneers, and three battalions of the 1st regiment, with a rocket battery composed it.

Colonel Glyn commanded the 3rd Column, and Rorke's Drift was the point selected for the crossing of this body of troops. It consisted of six guns of the Royal Artillery, one squadron of mounted infantry, the 24th regiment, 200 Natal volunteers, 150 mounted police, the second battalion of the 3rd regiment, with pioneers, native contingent, and a company of Royal Engineers.

No. 4 Column, under Colonel (afterwards Sir Evelyn) Wood, V.C., was to advance on the Blood River. Its strength was made up of Royal Artillery, the 13th regiment, 90th regiment, frontier light horse, and 200 of the native contingent,

In addition to the four columns, a fifth, under Colonel Rowlands, composed of the 80th regiment and mounted irregulars, was available. The total fighting force numbered some 7,000 British and 9,000 native troops—16,000 in all, with drivers. The Zulu Army was estimated at not less than 40,000 strong.

Probably no campaign has ever opened so disastrously for British arms as that which was undertaken against Cetewayo in January, 1879. At first sight, all appeared easy enough. Preparations were made upon a complete scale. Both transport and means of communication were regarded as highly satisfactory, and the first movements were conducted with success, and the two centre columns, Nos. 2 and 3, crossed the Tugela in safety, and effected their proposed junction in front of Rorke's Drift. Many cattle and sheep were captured in these first skirmishes of the campaign, and some few Zulus were killed with but slight loss on the British side.

On the morning of the 22nd January information came to hand of the presence of a large Zulu Army in front of the two centre columns, and Lord Chelmsford himself, with the greater portion of his force, advanced to clear the way. A force consisting of five companies of the 1st, battalion 24th regiment, a company of the 2nd battalion, with two guns, 104 mounted colonials, and 800 natives were left to guard the camp at Isandhlwana, which contained a valuable convoy of supplies. It was 1.30 a.m. or thereabouts when the advance columns with Lord Chelmsford left camp, coming first into contact with the enemy at about five miles distant. Till about 8 am. nothing happened in camp worthy of notice. About this time, however, detachments of Zulus were noticed coming in from the north-east, and immediately the force got under arms.

Slowly the Zulus began to work round to the rear of the British camp, and very shortly the 24th regiment found themselves surrounded. At this point the camp followers and native troops fled as best they could, the Zulus killing with the *assegai* all they could lay hands on. In a little while the British ware entirely overwhelmed.

Says Miss Colenso:—

After this period (1.30 p.m.) no one living escaped from Isandhlwana, and it is supposed the troops? had broken, and falling into confusion, all had perished after a brief struggle.

One bright incident alone stands out distinctly on this fatal 22nd January. On the storming of the camp by the Zulus, Lieutenants Melville and Coghill rode from the camp with the colours of their regiment. On they spurred in their frantic flight to the Tugela, and Coghill safely stemmed the torrent and landed on the farther shore. Melville, however, while in midstream, lost his horse, but clinging to the beloved colours, battled with the furious torrent with all the energy of despair. The Zulus pressed upon them.

Quick as thought, Coghill put his charger once more into the current, and struggled to the assistance of his brother officer, and, despite the fact that a Zulu bullet made short work of his horse, the two devoted men succeeded in making their escape with the colours still in their hands. The respite was not for long, however. Soon the yelling hordes were upon them, and, fighting fiercely to the last, Lieutenants Melville and Coghill died bravely upholding the honour of their country.

Meantime the advance party had pushed forward, and came in touch now and again with the enemy, who ever fell back before them, till about midday, when it was determined to return to camp. About this time word came to hand of heavy firing near the camp, and returning gradually till about six o'clock, when at a distance of only two miles from the waggons, "four men were observed slowly advancing towards the returning force. Thinking them to be enemy, fire was opened, and one of the men fell. The others ran into the open, holding up their hands, to show themselves unarmed." They proved to be the only survivors of the native contingent. "The camp was found tenanted by those who were taking their last long sleep."

Nearly 4,000 Zulus were found dead in the neighbourhood of Isandhlwana, showing the stout resistance made by our men. But, at the best, the disaster was a fearful one, the total Imperial losses being put at over 800 officers and men.

The night of the 22nd January saw another historic incident of the war the heroic defence of Rorke's Drift. At this important ford of the Tugela, vital to the British lines of communication, were stationed Lieutenants Chard and Bromhead, and B company, 2nd battalion 24th regiment. One hundred and thirty-nine men in all constituted the numbers of this devoted band. A mission station, one building of which was used as a hospital, and one as a commissariat store, made up Rorke's Drift.

At 3.15 p.m. (the time has been noted with great accuracy), Lieutenant Chard, who was down by the river, heard the sound of furious galloping. Louder and louder grew the hoof-beats, and ere long two spent and almost beaten horsemen drew sudden rein upon the Zulu

Zulu attack at Ulundi

bank of the Tugela. Wildly they demanded to be ferried across, and in a few frenzied words told the terrible tale of Isandhlwana. The Zulus were coming, they cried, and not a moment was to be lost!

One of them, Lieutenant Adendorf, remained behind to aid in the defence; the other was despatched post haste to Helpmakaar, the next point in the communications, to warn the troops and bring up reinforcements. Rorke's Drift must be held at whatever cost and against any odds! With feverish, but well-directed haste, all hands set to work to put the mission buildings into a state of defence. Mr. Dalton, of the Commissariat Department, assisted ably in the work that every man now tackled with a will. Loopholes were made in the buildings, and by means of two waggons and walls of mealie bags, they were connected and provisioned with the stores.

At this time, between 4 and 4.30 p.m., an officer of Dumford's Horse, with about 100 men, arrived, but these being totally spent, were sent on to Helpmakaar, and the Rorke's Drift garrison prepared cheerfully to face the foe. They were not long in coming. Whilst Lieutenant Chard was in the midst of constructing "an inner work of biscuit boxes, already two boxes high," about 4.30 p.m., the first of the enemy, some 600, appeared in sight. Rushing up to within fifty yards of the now extended position, they yelled defiance at the defenders, but a heavy fire from the loopholed masonry gave them pause at once.

From now on, the defence of Rorke's Drift became one prolonged and watchful struggle. Again, and again the frenzied Zulus threw themselves against the slender defences of the gallant band, and again and again were they hurled back, now with rifle fire, now with bayonet, but ever backward. Darkness set in, and still the rushes continued, till at length it was found necessary to retreat into the inner line of defence composed of the biscuit-boxes aforementioned.

At length the enemy succeeded in setting the hospital on fire, and the awful task of removing the sick, under the fearful odds, was taken in hand. Alas! not all could be removed, and many perished. No effort, however, was spared to get them all out, and at the last, with ammunition all expended, Privates Williams, Hook, R. Jones, and W. Jones held the door with the bayonet against the Zulu horde.

Now and again the battered entrenchments were repaired with mealie bags, and still the unequal fight went on. By midnight the little band was completely surrounded, and the light of the burning hospital, showing off garrison and assailants, revealed the awful struggle that was going on in the lurid light. "Never say die!" was the principle of the garrison, and it was carried out to the letter.

At 4 a.m. on the 23rd January the Zulu fire slackened, and by day-break the enemy was out of sight. Hand grasped hand, as it was slowly realised that the foe were beaten back and the flag was still fluttering over the gallant garrison. Even now Lieutenant Chard, nearly dead beat as was he and were all his men, relaxed no effort, and the work of repairing the defences went forward. Not without cause, for about 7 a.m. more Zulus appeared upon the hills to the south-west, but about an hour later No. 3 Column arrived upon the spot, and the enemy fell back. Seventeen killed and ten wounded were the casualties of the little garrison, while more than 350 Zulus lay dead around the mission station. At one time the number of the attacking force was estimated at 3,000.

Rorke's Drift, however, apart, the disaster to the British at Isand-hlwana was paralysing in its effect upon not only the colony of Natal, but the home country. The outcry against. Lord Chelmsford was bitter in both places. He was accused of having neglected the simple precautions which the Boers had always adopted in fighting with the Zulus, and which had been observed in our own campaigns against the Kaffirs. Though the silent celerity, the cunning, and the reckless bravery of the foe were well known, the camp at Isandhlwana had been pitched in a site singularly exposed and indefensible; it had not been protected even by a single trench, nor were the waggons "*laagered*." The arrangements for scouting had permitted a large Zulu force to assemble un-perceived.

The small party in Natal of which the Bishop of Colenso may be regarded as the leader, argued that Sir Bartle Frere had not only commenced an unjust war, but had commenced it with inadequate resources. Other parties declared it to be a military accident which ordinary prudence could not have foreseen.

Panic, however, reigned for a season in Natal. Mr. Archibald Forbes, the special correspondent of the *Daily News*, wrote in a graphic description of the situation which appeared on May 7, 1879:—

It is impossible to imagine a more critical situation than that now existing round the frontier of Zululand. The British territory lies at the mercy of the Zulus.

With such a state of affairs, the pacific intentions of King Cet-ewayo were never more clearly shown than at the present juncture, when he failed to press home the advantage his people had already won. Instead, the king once more made overtures of peace. One message ran:—

Cetewayo, sees no reason for the war which is being waged against him, and he asks, the government to appoint a place at which a conference could be held, with a view to the conclusion of peace.

Added to such messages as these the government expressed, through Sir Stafford Northcote, its anxiety "to promote an early and reasonable pacification of South Africa."

Miss Colenso's observations at this juncture are emphatic in the extreme:—

The High Commissioner's (Sir Bartle Frere's) habit of finding evil motives for every act of the Zulu king, made the case of the latter hopeless from the first.

Be these things as they may, the war, once begun, was carried on but under new auspices.

With a feeling of relief, the public learned, on May 26th, that Sir Garnet Wolseley had been sent out to South Africa to take command of the forces, and to conduct, as the Queen's Commissioner, the Governments of Natal and the Transvaal, and our relations with the Zulus. In making this appointment, the government were careful to explain that no slight, either upon Sir Bartle Frere or Lord Chelmsford was intended, but that "an arrangement by which the chief civil and military authority at the seat of war was distributed among several persons, could no longer be deemed adequate." On June 28th, Sir Garnet Wolseley arrived in Natal.

Meanwhile, the other columns of the expedition had been operating with more or less success elsewhere. On the day of Isandhlwana, Colonel Pearson's column had been engaged against an *impi* of 5,000 Zulus, ten miles south of Ekowe, and defeated them with heavy lose. With 1,200 men he then prepared to hold the carefully-entrenched position he had selected round the mission buildings at Ekowe. In a very brief space of time, he found himself cut off from his communications, and hemmed in on all sides by the enemy.

By means of heliograph signals communication was kept up by the beleaguered force and Fort Tenedos, the base of relief on the Tugela, and by this means it was soon ascertained that towards the end of March the defenders would be hard pressed for provisions. Relief was accordingly hurried forward, and on the 29th of the month a column of 4,000 British troops fresh from England, and 2,000 natives, started from the Tugela. Every possible precaution was observed by Lord Chelmsford, who commanded in person. At early dawn on the 2nd April, Colonel Pearson flashed intelligence to the relieving force that the enemy were approaching.

The Zulus swept on with their usual reckless valour, and were met with a perfect hail of lead and fire, gatlings and rocket batteries being used with deadly effect. Again and again, they renewed the onset, but "never got nearer than twenty yards to the shelter trenches," and after an hour and a half of splendid fight, they broke and fled. The cavalry cut down the fugitives, and of their force of 10,000, 1,500 lay dead upon the field. This engagement at Gingihlovo, resulting in the relief of Colonel Pearson, cost us but a trifling loss.

Elsewhere, Colonels Wood and Rowlands had joined hands, and were pressing Umbilini, the Swazi chief, who had succeeded in cutting up some 45 men of the 80th regiment while sleeping in camp on the Intombi River. Colonel Wood, on March 28th, captured this chief's stronghold at Hlobani, but while returning to his camp with many captured cattle, was trapped by the whole Zulu *impi*, and, on the following day, his camp at Kambula was attacked by 20,000 Zulus. For four hours a desperate fight ensued, but finally the enemy were driven off. Soon after this Umbilini himself was killed.

The tide of war now turned. By the 15th April all the British reinforcements had arrived, and the invasion of the enemy's country, deferred by Isandhlwana, was again considered. Ulundi, as before, the king's chief *kraal*, was the objective of the expedition, and much time was yet spent in getting together supplies for the large force now about to be employed, and in considering the route it was to take.

The interval now elapsing was conspicuous for an occurrence which threw a gloom over the whole field force, and even the continent of Europe itself.

On June 2nd, the young Prince Imperial of France, who had been allowed to proceed to South Africa, largely as a spectator of the military operations, was sent with a small escort of troopers to examine the proposed line of march from the Itilezi Hill. Lieutenant Carey of the 98th went with him. Ever eager in adventure, and careless of personal risk, the prince insisted upon setting out with only a portion of his escort, the others not having turned out in time. The discovery of a good water supply for the next camping ground was the object of the reconnaissance.

Never for a moment supposing that the prince and Lieutenant Carey would proceed far without the Basuto members of their escort, whose extraordinary powers of sight and hearing rendered them invaluable on such an occasion, Colonel Harrison and Major Grenfell rode back after a certain distance. The others went on alone. About 3 p.m. the little party halted at a deserted *kraal*, deciding to leave again in an hour's time, but before the hour was over the native guide came hastening in to say that a Zulu had been sighted coming over the hill. The prince never foolhardy, at once gave the order to "Mount!" But the Zulus were quicker.

Firing a volley from the mealies, which grew high on every side, they rushed down, *assegai* in hand. All succeeded in mounting but the prince, whose spirited grey charger would not be controlled. In a moment he was alone, on foot, surrounded by the savage foe. Turning round, on seeing his riderless horse, several of the troopers saw the prince running towards them on foot. "Not a man turned back. They galloped wildly on." Some distance later they met Colonels Wood and Buller, and to them they made the melancholy report.

Next day, General Marshall, with a cavalry patrol, went out to search for the prince, and lying in a *donga*, 200 yards from the *kraal*, they found his body, stripped bare, with the exception of a gold chain and cross which he wore round his neck. There were no less than eighteen *assegai* wounds in the body, every one of them in front, as he had died fearless to the last and facing the relentless foe. The bodies of two troopers were found some distance away; they had been killed in their flight.

The historian of the war says:—

What citizen of Maritzburg, will ever forget the melancholy Sunday afternoon, cold and storm-laden, when, at the first distant sound of the sad approaching funeral music, all left their homes and lined the streets through which the violet-adorned coffin passed on its way to its temporary resting place?

Transferred at Durban to the flagship of Commodore Richards, the *Boadicea*, and thence, at Simons Bay to H.M.S. *Orontes*, the body of the gallant boy was brought to England with every mark of sorrow and respect. Lieutenant Carey was found by court-martial to be guilty of misbehaviour before the enemy, but military opinion condemned the verdict, and on his arrival in England he was released from arrest. All ranks and all classes were profoundly sympathetic towards the prince's mother, the ex-Empress Eugenie.

In this interval of waiting also, the bodies of those who died at Isandhlwana were at length interred, the 24th regiment burying its own dead before the assembled battalions.

Once more Cetewayo was reported to be eager to submit, and on June 30th chiefs of rank arrived at Lord Chelmsford's camp, bearing elephants' tusks, the Zulu symbol of good faith. They were told that the British Army would advance to a position on the left bank of the Umoolori River, and there, halt, if certain conditions were complied with. These were that the two seven-pounders captured at Isandhlwana and the captured cattle, should be restored by chiefs of authority, and one of his regiments should come and lay down its arms.

By noon on July 3rd these demands were not complied with, and some of our men who went down to the river to water were fired on by the Zulus. On July 4 the whole force crossed the river at 6.45 a.m. and advanced towards Ulundi. Streams of Zulus soon appeared on every side. The cavalry on the right and left became engaged two hours later, and slowly retiring as the enemy advanced, passed into "the square," which had been drawn up in a singularly advantageous position. The enemy advanced in loose formation, throwing out, however, the customary "horns" of the Zulu *impi*. Then, when the distance was sufficiently reduced, the fire of the infantry commenced.

The enemy fired rapidly, but, as usual, with little effect. The British artillery fire was tremendous. Volley after volley swept through the Zulu ranks as they rushed boldly in to the attack, but the issue was not long. The devoted "braves "began to waver, and the ripe moment was seized upon by Lord Chelmsford. The cavalry swept out of the square, which opened to let them through, and within an hour the Zulus were in full retreat. The 17th Lancers wrought tremendous execution, killing and riding down in all directions. No less than 150 of the enemy fell before this squadron alone.

Brief, as described, was the Battle of Ulundi, which terminated the Zulu campaign. The credit of the victory admittedly belongs to Lord Chelmsford, who thus regained much of the prestige which he had forfeited at Isandhlwana.

The British lost 10 killed at Ulundi; the Zulus nearly 1,000. Our force numbered 4,000 Europeans and 1,100 natives; the Zulus counted 20,000 in all.

Later in the day the army advanced to Ulundi, burnt it with all

The 17th Lancers in the Zulu War

the other military *kraals* and returned to camp. Nearly all the leading chiefs in Zululand marked the victory by their submission.

Cetewayo himself, footsore and weary, was run to earth on the morning of August 28th in a *kraal* near the Black Umoolosi. The *kraal* was surrounded, and the king bidden to come forth. Cetewayo, creeping out, stood with kingly composure and defiance among the dragoons. He was taken by sea to Cape Town and there confined in the castle. He was a man of splendid physique, and, says a writer, "showed good-humoured resignation." He took to European clothes, and was photographed.

The terms of peace were subsequently dictated by Sir Garnet Wolseley at Ulundi, on the 1st September—the anniversary day of Cetewayo's coronation.

CHAPTER 13

The Battle of Mazra: 1880

The Battle of Mazra, one of the stiffest of the many battles between Britain and Afghanistan, was the deciding blow in a campaign with a curious history.

About 1878, hostilities were very pronounced in Afghanistan against Britain, and, as a result of these, the *ameer*, who appeared unnerved at the troubles, abdicated the throne. This action after a time was consented to, General Roberts temporarily taking over the supreme control.

While Britain was casting about for someone qualified to fill the position of *ameer*, Abdurrahman Khan appeared on the scene. Abdurrahman was the son of Afzool, and nephew of the *ameer*, Sheer Ali. He had taken a prominent part in the rebellions formed by his father and uncle against the *ameer*. This prince entered the country with a few followers, and in the belief that, from the capacity he had displayed during Sheer Ali's time, he was likely to make a good ruler, negotiations were opened up with him on behalf of the British Government. Eventually he accepted the position of *ameer*, and was installed at Cabul.

While these events had been taking place in and about Cabul, Ayoob Khan, the brother of Yakoob Khan, who had been deposed, was at Herat. During Sheer Ali's rule, Yakoob Khan and Ayoob Khan had together governed Herat independently of their father, and as soon as it became known to Ayoob that the Indian Government had resolved not to place Yakoob Khan on the *musnud* of Cabul, he began making preparations to assert, by force of arms, his own claim to the *ameership*.

The intention of the new claimant was to make an advance on Kandahar, the capital, and it was as a result of the success of this movement that the Battle of Mazra had ultimately to be fought. During several months Ayoob, with fixed determination, occupied himself in making arrangement for the advance on Kandahar, and so satisfactorily had these been accomplished that by the 9th June, 1880, he was ready to form his camp outside the walls of Herat, preparatory to a march forward. The town of Herat is situated about 367 miles from Kandahar, and, as a matter of fact, the Indian Government was somewhat sceptical as to Ayoob's capability of marching an army so far. Nevertheless, he did it, with what results we shall see.

About the 12th June the claimant commenced his march. His army at starting consisted of 2,500 cavalry, of whom only 900 were regulars, the rest being *Khazadars*, or mounted militia; ten regiments of infantry, varying in strength from 350 to 500 men; and 5 batteries, including one mule battery, with about 30 guns. Roughly, he had altogether between 7,000 and 8,000 men, and when it is remembered how hardy and resolute the average Afghan is, this in itself was a fairly formidable enemy that had set its mask towards the capital of Kandahar.

Hearing of the advance of Ayoob, British forces were at once posted to various parts of the country to obstruct the journey forward, but it was not to be; for, as was afterwards discovered, the unusual precedent was to present itself to Britain of her beginning a campaign in very bad fashion and finishing up brilliantly.

We have already referred to the strength of the forces which Ayoob Khan was to lead, and with these he made splendid progress on his journey to the capital. The obstructions which were put in his way were easily overcome, and the defeat of General Burrows was one of Ayoob's greatest triumphs of the campaign.

By about 20th July Kandahar was occupied by about 4,000 British troops, and on the 9th August General Roberts, according to orders, started his famous march from Cabul to relieve Kandahar.

About this time Ayoob Khan's army was considerably strengthened by *Ghilzais*, having an army then under his control of nearly 20,000. But the real crisis was only brewing, and the splendid skill and resource of that ablest of British generals, Sir Frederick Roberts, was soon to be rewarded in the splendid triumph of Mazra.

The arrangements made by General Roberts prior to setting out on his famous mission to Kandahar, were of the most complete order, and he led in round numbers fully 10,000 troops to the scene of hostilities. Of these, close on 2,000 were Europeans, and 8,000 camp followers. General Roberts took with him a certain amount of European stores, such as rum, tea, and five days' flour, but trusted largely for other supplies to the food and forage to be obtained on the line of march. But even, this was not left to chance, and to facilitate the general's obtaining such supplies, the *ameer* sent with him several chiefs.

It was indeed a curious sight as the troops plodded onward, eager for the fray, for, in view of the difficulty of the road, the general took no wheeled vehicles with him, and even the guns were mounted on mules and elephants. But the commander's foresight as to the difficulties he would have to encounter did not end here, and knowing that the ordinary road for supplies might be exhausted by the previous passage of troops and the presence of large bodies of insurgents, he changed from this route, and marched by the Logur Valley, which had been comparatively untouched. Although this road had the small disadvantage of hindering a couple of days longer the progress of the army by the ordinary route, it brought him into contact with the latter again a short distance before reaching Ghuzni. Here some opposition was anticipated, but, notwithstanding, none was experienced, and the army continued its march unmolested.

General Roberts accomplished this march, which must, reckoning his detour, have been little less than 370 miles, without any opposition, in 24 days, being an average of 14½ miles a day. Considering the difficulties that had to be encountered on the way, this was splendid progress. Picking up the garrison of 1,100 men at Khelat-i-ghilzai, he arrived at Kandahar on August 31. Here was a feat almost unparalleled in history, and reflecting the highest credit on the troops, and their skilful, gallant and energetic commander.

The news of General Roberts' approach soon spread, and Ayoob Khan, knowing well apparently what he had to face in furtherance of his desires before referred to, at once made an effort to open communications with him. General Roberts, however, having in view the whole situation and the nature of the negotiations, was entirely against this course, and would hear of nothing but unconditional surrender from the other side, and also the surrender of such prisoners as had been previously taken in the course of engagements.

The general then proceeded to encamp, and prepared for the coming battle. Passing round the northern wall of Kandahar, he encamped between the city and the enemy's position. The British general was continually on the alert, and in the determination not to leave a stone unturned to accomplish his purpose, he immediately sent out his cavalry to reconnoitre. The main reason for this action was the fear that the Afghans, after hearing of the way their leader's attempt at negotiations had been received, would retreat without fighting, and thus prolong the trouble, another prominent reason being General

Roberts' repeated experience of the moral effect of a prompt blow. In furtherance of his designs, Roberts determined to give battle the very next day.

During the first week in August, Ayoob, fresh from his victories elsewhere, directed his main body to appear in front of the city, his cavalry having invested it several days previously. Still watchful and on the alert, his method of going about matters was extremely guarded. He had erected batteries and occupied villages and posts on every side save the north. Up to the time of the approach of General Roberts, however, he did not venture on more than annoying the town, with a distant and desultory cannonade, and the occupation, chiefly by the armed peasants and Ghazis, of a few posts near the walls.

On the other hand, the citadel was occupied in great force, and the garrison felt confident that they could defend their position against all Ayoob's attacks. In an attempt, however, by one of the British generals, General Primrose, to impede the progress of the besiegers, the British troops lost heavily. The garrison set about the work of repairing the fortifications and otherwise taking every opportunity to make their position as strong as possible.

Returning to General Roberts' decision to strike a prompt blow, the result of the cavalry reconnaissance and the general's own personal examination was the plan that we will mention after describing the position taken up by Ayoob Khan more minutely. About three miles from the north-west angle from the city of Kandahar is a range of heights running from southwest to north-east. Parallel to this range, and at a distance from its crest varying between one and three-quarters and two and three-quarters miles flows the Argaridub, which, by the way, is almost everywhere fordable at the end of August. In the intervening valley are many villages, enclosures, and gardens.

Towards the south-west, or the enemy's right, the range is terminated rather abruptly by a hill about 1,000 feet above the level of Kandahar. This hill, called the Pir Paimal, is joined to the rest of the range by a *col* or *neck*, over which passes the road leading from the north-west angle of the city to the valley of the Helmund, in which is situated, at a distance of about four miles, the village of Mazra. Here, after a close scrutiny of his position, Ayoob had determined to establish his standing camp and headquarters.

The pass above mentioned is called Baba-wali Pass, and provided the advantage of leading directly to the centre of the enemy's advanced position, which was on both sides of the road. The front of the pass is screened from the city by an isolated hill, lower than the range in front. In front of Pir Paimal and to its right rear are situated several villages. In rear of the position again, and covering the village of Mazra from an enemy advancing up the river is a detached hill. It was on the crest of the main ridge of this, that guns had been mounted, and, taking into consideration the arrangement of Ayoob's camp, the leader of the Afghans was evidently expecting a front attack.

On the other hand, General Roberts' plan of operations was entirely in contrast, and was yet simple, effective and safe. In the first place, the general resolved to amuse the enemy by demonstrations by General Primrose with a part of the Kandahar garrison against the Baba-wali Pass. Secondly, he sent General Gough's cavalry to the river at the entrance to the valley, to turn the enemy's right with the three infantry brigades of the Cabul-Kandahar force. The whole scheme was worked out with admirable foresight, and thoughtful resource.

At nine o'clock in the morning of 1st September the battle began. According to instructions, General Primrose made demonstrations against the Baba-wali Pass, and fired with his heavy battery at the troops occupying it. The ruse succeeded well, and attention was fixed for the time on Primrose and his attempted attack.

It was recorded by one of the officers of Primrose's forces that this trick on the part of General Roberts succeeded in a greater degree than was really expected, and, as the enemy appeared to be entirely deluded by it, the British forces were encouraged on seeing that the very initial part of the proceedings pointed to complete success. Primrose having thus attracted the enemy's attention, General Roberts next despatched Cough's cavalry brigade to the Argaridab, where it was favourably placed, either to cut off a retreat towards Girishk or to carry out a pursuit up the valley.

Simultaneous with this, he gave the order to the infantry, commanded by General Ross, to advance. All the forces were now in action, and the battle had commenced in real earnest. One eye-witness of the scene stated that the spectacle of the forces marching towards each other was one of the most impressive of many campaigns. The first of the brigades to come into collision with the Afghans was General Macpherson's of the 1st Brigade.

In front of Macpherson, and a little in advance of the right of Pir Paimal Hill, was an elevated and strongly-occupied village. This village was heavily shelled by the British artillery for a time with steady effect, and the enemy made an effectual reply. Gradually the opposing forces seemed to be wavering, and, observing this cringing, the 92nd Highlanders and the 2nd Goorkhas rushed on and stormed the village in most gallant fashion.

The bravery displayed by these regiments was splendid, and in determined fashion they forced the enemy out of their position. The 2nd, or Baker's, Brigade then came into line with the 1st, the 3rd, or Macgregor's, Brigade being in support. These two brigades were making for Pir Paimal, but they were to encounter stubborn resistance.

On the way, a number of orchards and enclosures had to be passed through, and here the enemy, showing in great numbers, fought desperately and well. Great forces of the Afghans came out of hiding, and, as the brigades appeared, rushed on them in overwhelming numbers, forming a formidable attack. As a great show of fight was anticipated, however, the brigades never rallied a moment, and nothing could resist the heroic onslaught which they made to win the day. The Afghans, with admirable foresight, had prepared thoroughly for any attack that might be made upon them in turn, and, besides occupying every available covert, they also lined every wall.

The Afghans, as indeed most Orientals, are an exceedingly formidable foe when under cover, and at the outset they absolutely refused to give ground to the fire. It was only to the repeated rushes of the brigades that they yielded, and it was here that the British losses were greatest. But the British attempt was shortly to be successful. Natives and Europeans vied with each other in courage, and cut the enemy off at every corner. Forcing their way on, the brigades made great progress, and were ultimately successful in their desire to capture Pir Paimal.

The resistance still shown by the Afghans was characteristic of the race, and, although falling in large numbers, there was a determination goading them on almost equal to that prevailing on our side. From Pir Paimal the infantry continued to push on notwithstanding the desperate attempts of the enemy to hold their ground. Pressing the Afghans still further from their position, two of their camps and several pieces of artillery fell into the hands of the brigades, and here there was a perceptible slackening of the resistance on the part of Ayoob's army.

It is one of the most wonderful things in war to note to what extent an apparently trifling occurrence will turn the scales of fortune.

Up to this time, although the British force had certainly had the best of matters, in that they had made good progress, the Afghan Army had never belied their reputation as a daring, if not foolhardy, race. But at this stage, when so little lay between the armies in regard to

A BATTLE IN AFGHANISTAN

the main issue, the inevitable hitch was to occur and spoil the ultimate prospect of an Afghan victory. It was only a slight hitch, to be sure, but it was sufficient to create a much wider breach, and after the British brigades had been successful in making the small capture noted above, an extraordinary alarm began to spread along the enemy's line, and soon the flight became general. The whole of the Afghan forces retreated before the British infantry in the utmost confusion, leaving behind all ammunition and so on in their flight. The infantry, much exhausted as a result of their heavy work, pursued the retreating forces, picking up guns at almost every step.

By noon, Ayoob's standing camp at Mazra was in our hands, and the battle was over. The enemy was completely routed. But while the infantry were thoroughly exhausted with their morning's work, the cavalry, which up till now had largely participated only as spectators, at this juncture began to play a vital part in the issue. With his fine body of horsemen, Gough waited his opportunity, and, as soon as he saw the chance, dashed forward and crossed the river to where the fugitives were fleeing in retreat. The sight of the enemy with the cavalry in chase was in entire contrast with that which had been witnessed an hour before.

The pursuit of the cavalry at the heels of the retreating Afghans was continued over a great distance at a terrific pace in the direction of the valley of Khakrey to the north, till the pursuing body, getting even with their quarry, succeeded in sabring between 200 and 300 of them. By this time the Afghans were utterly fatigued, but, scattering on all sides, many managed to get clear of their pursuers. The main object of Gough's dash forward—that of dispersing the enemy on all sides—had been satisfactorily accomplished, and, making a complete circuit, he afterwards returned to camp.

On the way back Gough's forces joined the 3rd Bombay cavalry and 3rd Scinde Horse, under General Nuttal, so that had any mishap occurred in Gough's pursuit of the enemy, these other forces would have yet saved disaster. General Nuttal, during the hottest part of the fighting, had been stationed with his brigade at Baba-wali Pass. When General Roberts saw the enemy was breaking, Nuttal and his forces were brought through the Pass, and ordered to carry on the pursuit for no less than fifteen miles up the river. In the course of his chase, Nuttal was successful in cutting up more than a hundred of the fugitives, and, like Gough, completely dispersed the enemy in flight.

The loss of the enemy in this battle, one of the stiffest in the history of Afghanistan, were severe. The killed alone would probably be upwards of 1,200. A study of the figures as regards the work done, shows the havoc played by the respective British forces. Thus, on the direct line of the infantry advance no fewer than 650 dead bodies were found, while between 300 and 400 were slain by the cavalry in pursuit, many corpses never being recovered. This in itself shows that the attack on all hands by the British forces had been a deadly one, and was in most instances followed by disaster to Ayoob's army.

In the action itself Ayoob lost some 32 guns, and six others, including two captured by General Burrows, were afterwards brought in, thus completing the total number of pieces possessed by the Afghan leader on the morning of 1st September, when the battle began. The general nature of the flight is here strongly evidenced. Not only was Ayoob's army completely dispersed in every direction, but also completely cowed, while he himself, a discredited man without any political future, made the best of his way to Herat.

The only drawback, if such it can be called, to the entire success of this action, was that the Afghans got away too easily. For, in point of fact, the cavalry, from the difficulty of their positions, were unable to inflict the crushing blow upon the retreating forces that they might otherwise have done if better situated. Nevertheless, it has to be recognised that if the infantry had been so greatly fatigued there could have been no flight. For we have seen how desperate the Afghans were in their attempts to gain a victory, while the main object of the cavalry's pursuit, that of dispersing the enemy, was yet successfully accomplished.

The total number of casualties in General Roberts' force was only a little over 200—surely a small price to pay for so brilliant and decisive a victory.

The real cause of the enemy's flight, the incident recorded about the taking of two of their camps, was greatly aided, it is supposed, by the spirit of dissension in the Afghan ranks. As to Ayoob himself, there was no want of skill on the part of his advisers, no matter what the ultimate result was. Ayoob himself was not a man of much ability or force of character, but it was evident all along that he had some excellent military counsellors with him.

In the papers relating to this campaign presented to the Houses of Parliament, the very important statement was made as a matter of fact that never had an army been handled with more skill than was Ayoob's during its brief and ultimately disastrous campaign. Such a statement, coming from such a source, goes far to prove that the acumen shown in things military on the part of the Afghan leader was not a little remarkable. His advances to the scene of the final battle were conducted most methodically, and in accordance with all the rules of war. Indeed, the generalship of Ayoob, and the conduct of his troops were such that the conviction got abroad that the operations had been directed, and the guns worked, under the supervision of Europeans, although no proof of this could be obtained.

The Battle of Majuba Hill: 1881

By James Grant

On the evening of the 26th of February, there were detailed in the camp for a secret expedition, 180 Gordon Highlanders, 150 of the 58th, 150 of the 2nd 60th Rifles, and 65 bluejackets, under Commander Romilly, too slender and too mixed a force for the work in hand, as a few hours proved. These men paraded in dead silence close by Sir George Colley's tent at nine o'clock, after the bugles had blown the "last post," with seventy-five rounds of ammunition in their pouches—545 bayonets in all, exclusive of Army Hospital Corps, Staff, &c Had these 545 been of one corps, led by their own officers, even in these days, when our military cohesion seems a thing of the past, the result might have been different, and Majuba Hill might have been held till our reserves came on later next day, and then the Boers would have been placed between two fires.

Again, were shoulder to shoulder in war, the men of the Gordon Highlanders with those of the old Rutlandshire, as their predecessors had been, when, in Egypt, they fought around the Tower of Mandora, but alas! no laurels were to be gathered now as then, under the guidance of the gallant Abercrombie.

The order was given in low tones, and not another word was spoken, as the column moved out of camp at ten o'clock, in sections of fours, with rifles at the "trail"—but passive obedience and silence are still the characteristics of the British soldier. The destination was kept a profound secret till the moment of starting, and then it became known, that the point to be attained was the high hill on the left of the *nek*, known as the Spitzkop or Majuba—the former name being descriptive of a sugar-loaf or peaked hill—and that it was intended to take the Boer position in flank.

As long as our soldiers think they are going to fight, they care little where the field or the foe may be; but on this occasion, the staff could not help remarking that poor Sir George Colley looked, as one described it, "tired, careworn, and haggard, as he marched along in silence at the head of the column."

He said to the correspondent of the *Standard*:

> I mean to take the hill, and should the enemy attempt to cut me off, the 2nd 60th and the Hussars are within call at Newcastle. We are taking three days' rations with us, and before these are finished, we ought to be thoroughly secure.

There are two lofty hills—one directly on the left flank of the Boer position, the other nearer the *nek* and commanding it. A ridge connects them both.

The night was pitchy dark at first, and the march across a country unknown to the men, was toilsome in the extreme. At first the way was over comparatively level ground, but it was at the base of the hill the real difficulties began. Prior to this, there was a halt now and then, and the wavy outline of the Drakensberg could be traced, in deep black masses, against even the darkness of the sky. The path narrowed so much that after a time the sections of fours were diminished to Indian file, necessitating a sad delay, ere the summit could be attained.

At a precipitous part of the hill a company of Rifles was left, and at the base one of Highlanders. Their helmets were dyed brown now, but their colour came curiously out of the gloom. In their care the horses were left. These men were all ordered to set about entrenching themselves at once, while the remainder, just as day was nearly breaking, and they were already getting worn with a rough march of six hours, guided by Kaffirs, began the ascent, a work of terrible toil, as in many places the ground was most precipitous, the men having to crawl on their hands and knees, up *dongas* and over boulders, dragging their rifles after them, as best they could, up ways that even mountaineers might have shrunk from in open daylight

Ever and *anon*, large stones and boulders, loosened by the feet of the climbers rolled thundering down into the obscurity below; and in some instances, when, after enormous labour, our soldiers thought they were at the top, they had to descend and veer to the right or left before ascending again; and but for the native guides, though sometimes at fault, the summit would never have been attained. The task would have been one of toil to unencumbered men; but to soldiers armed, accoutred, and carrying their ammunition, water-bottles, and three days' provisions in their haversacks, it was painful in the extreme.

In some places prickly jungle and long grass had to be toiled through. At one part the foremost men were brought to a complete halt, on finding themselves opposed by a massive wall of smooth and slippery rock, totally bare of vegetation, causing a retrogression of some hundred yards to reach a pathway on the left—a mere gulley or water-course, encumbered by boulders; and by that route Colonel Stewart, Chief of the Staff, and a few of the foremost men reached the top, from whence they could see Laing's Nek, behind its dark crest, and the fires of the Boer encampment, in long dotted lines sparkling out, as lighted for their meal. The *nek* seemed about 1,500 yards below Majuba Hill; far away were the dark *kloofs* of the mighty Drakensberg, sunk in black-est shadow, and far down below rolled the broad bosom of the Buffalo River, its silvery haze expanding in the growing light of day.

Majuba Hill completely enfiladed the enemy's position, and had we had men enough to hold it, and, more than all, had cannon been there, Laing's Nek would speedily have been untenable.

To facilitate his exertions in the ascent, which at one point was barred by an almost impenetrable zone of the densest bush, the general had substituted for his military boots and spurs a pair of socks and slippers, and wore them throughout the subsequent engagement.

The first part of this desperate and most rash expedition was achieved. The summit of Majuba was won, and the troops found themselves in a spacious saucer-shaped plateau, about 1,000 yards in circuit, constituting a kind of natural circular breastwork, which they believed they were quite capable of defending, and all flattered them-selves that the success would be complete.

One already quoted says:

I was beside the general when he passed the word down for all the troops to come up. Although quiet and self-possessed, I still fancied that in his anxious and careworn countenance there were traces of deep and suppressed excitement. It was twenty minutes to four when the first men emerged on the summit of the mountain; but before the last had clambered up it was nearly five o'clock. In the interval, those of us who were first up lay down in the grass to snatch a half-hour's sleep.

The last sleep in life it proved to many! The general slept, too, and at a time when entrenchments should have been formed.

As the sun rose, and the Boers saw steel glittering on the summit of Majuba, and *anon* red-coats dotting its sky-line and overlooking their position, they were observed to rush from their fires into their *laager*, in evident rage and consternation. They were, at first, apparently struck with a panic; some were saddling and mounting their horses in hot haste; others were inspanning the teams to their waggons, as if about to retreat, and some had actually fled.

The troops were posted at intervals of ten paces between their files round the summit, each man making or discovering a little stone or turf defence to lie behind, while the Naval Brigade and fifty men of the 58th were placed as a reserve in the centre of the hollow. The fighting line was not exactly on the extreme brow of the hill, an error that proved fatal eventually. Already the men, after the toil of the past night, felt perishing with thirst, for their water-bottles were empty; but, fortunately, Lieutenant Hector Macdonald, of the Gordon Highlanders, dug a well, and struck upon water.

Meanwhile, on the slope and scarp of the mountain were the most admirable bits of cover skirmishers could desire; but, either from the smallness of the force or a misunderstanding as to the mode of defence, these were left untenanted 'till occupied by the Boers in their ascent; and from these very posts and points our men were shot through the head and chest when, to command them, they crossed over the crest above.

No order as to independent or other file-firing would seem to have been issued, and thus, as soon as the Boer *laager* became lit up by the sun, some of our younger soldiers began to take pot-shots at a party of mounted Boers, who were far beyond range!

"Silence those fellows at once!" said the general, when he heard the firing and began to consider the ammunition; but it was too late. Roused fully by the sound, the whole Boer force now got under arms, though wild confusion seemed to prevail in their camp. Men in hundreds were seen rushing up to man the entrenchments on the *nek*; others proceeded to drive in their grazing cattle and horses from the mountain slopes; while a number came furiously galloping round the base of the Majuba Hill, regardless of the fire that was opened on them, and, dismounting, crept out of sight to secret places, from whence, with deadly aim, they sent shot after shot upwards; and Sir George Colley passed an order round for the skirmishers only to fire when they had the enemy within practicable range.

During the subsequent hour wave after wave of Boer skirmishers came on round the left face of the hill to feed their fighting line, and disappeared beneath the slope, and at nine o'clock they opened a hot fire upon a part of the hill which was held by only twenty Gordon Highlanders under Lieutenant Ian Hamilton (instructor of musketry), who reported to the general that he suspected the Boers to be assembling in great strength under the giddy slope beneath his position, where they were, as yet, out of sight.

He was offered a reinforcement of twenty more Highlanders, but took only ten, and even with these he succeeded in checking the enemy's fire, while his men behaved with splendid coolness, delivering their fire only when a Boer's head became visible, and by twelve o'clock only four of themselves had been wounded, but these four still continued fighting.

Sometime before this, the general, with his staff and Commander Romilly, of the Naval Brigade, furnished by H.M.S. *Boadicea*, were standing on a part of the plateau which the enemy's fire had failed to reach, when suddenly a puff of smoke spouted from a clump of bushes about 900 yards down the hill. A shout rose from the group, and Commander Romilly was seen to roll over and over again on the ground, mortally wounded, by an explosive bullet it was affirmed, though, we believe, it had gone completely through his body. This incident, which occurred in full view of all, was not without a bad effect on our young soldiers, who saw that to be exposed to a Boer marksman at any possible range was certain destruction.

In their plan to cut off the force the Boers proceeded very methodically, and, surrounding the whole hill, maintained a constant fire, starring with lead the stones behind which our men lay, but more often dealing death among the latter. Still our men were cool and confident, and the possibility of the position being carried had not yet occurred to any of them.

Between twelve and one the Boers' fire began to slacken, and it actually seemed as if they were drawing off, which, however, was far from being the case, as it was soon found that they were strongly reinforcing their fighting line, and shortly after one a terrific fire, accompanied by shouts of triumph, suddenly burst forth from the lower slopes of the hill on the right, the side on which the firing had all along been very heavy, and a tremendous upward rush began to be made by the enemy.

The rocks and bushes, the tufts of *spekboom* and boulders on the slope, became suddenly alive with active and powerful Boers, in shovel-hats and leather trousers, grim, swarthy, and bearded colonists, leaping from crag to crag, jostling and pressing upward, with a hungry,

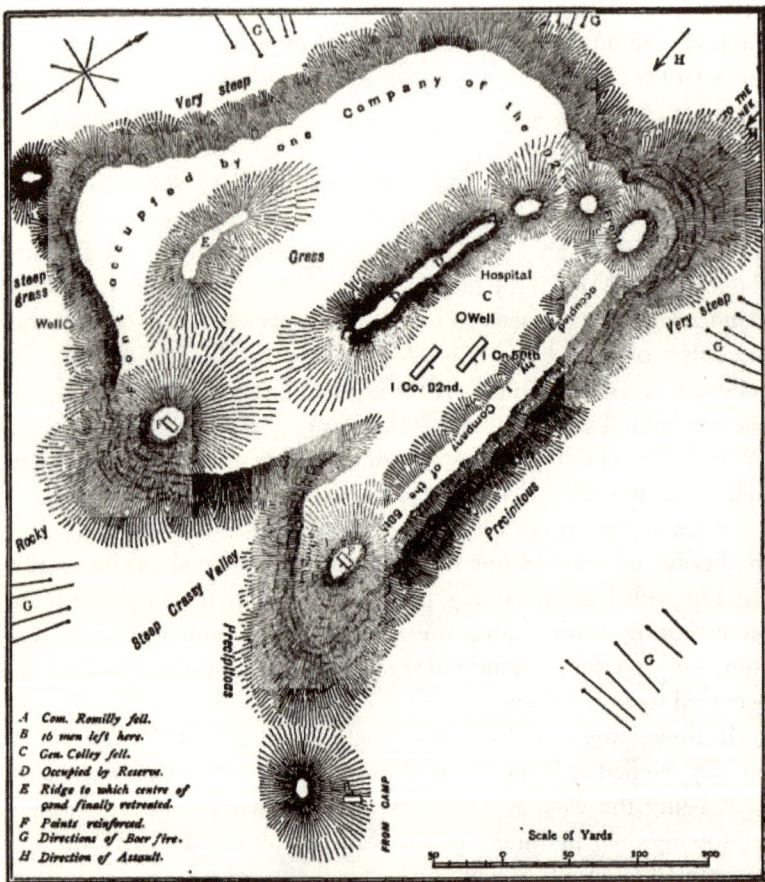

Very steep

Front occupied by one Company of the

C

G

H
TO THE NEK

steep
grass

Well

E

Grass

Hospital
C

O Well

On Spib.

I Co. D 2nd.

Company

of 60 Gds.

Precipitous

Rocky

G

Steep Grassy Valley

Precipitous

Very steep

G

G

FROM CAMP

A   Com. Romilly fell.
B   16 men left here.
C   Gen. Colley fell.
D   Occupied by Reserve.
E   Ridge to which centre of
    66nd finally retreated.
F   Points reinforced.
G   Directions of Boer fire.
H   Direction of Assault.

Scale of Yards
50   0   50   100   200

PLAN OF THE SUMMIT OF MAJUBA HILL (FEBRUARY 27, 1881).

blood-famished glare in their eyes, the very fever of battle, combined with the dogged look of men prepared to dare all—to do or die!

A hail of bullets was shrieking overhead and all around our men. The skirmishing line under Hamilton gave way, and all the rest became exposed to a desperate fusillade, and an evident recoil began. Lieutenant Ian MacDonald, of the 92nd Highlanders, a brave fellow, who had been promoted from the rank of colour-sergeant by Sir Frederick Roberts for brilliant valour at the Peiwar Kotal and the Battle of Charasiah, was now seen, revolver in hand, threatening to shoot down any man that passed him. Many did get away, and disappeared on the side of the hill next the camp, "but some 150 good men, mostly Highlanders, bluejackets, and old soldiers of the 58th, remained to man the ridge for a final stand," says the correspondent of the *Standard*, who afterwards came to be known as "Majuba" Cameron.

The fire these men received and gave was something awful. Thrice the Boers hurled their strength against them, and thrice they recoiled, and in the lulls of their firing our soldiers were heard crying to each other, "We'll not budge from this! We'll give them the bayonet if they come closer." Then Colour-Sergeant Fraser, of the Gordons, was shot down, with both legs shattered just below the kilt, with many of his comrades in the Afghan War, just as their career of long and glorious service was drawing to a close, and all that the manhood and devotion of this mixed band of seasoned men could do was but to stem the advancing torrent for a time.

"Hold your ground, my lads!" Colonel Stewart was heard to cry again and again to those who were wavering elsewhere.

"Now is the moment to give them the cold steel!" an impatient officer would cry.

"Not yet, not yet," the general is reported to have said.

The *Times* correspondent says:

The officers shouted, 'Rally on your right!' which would bring them to the left rear near the general with about fifty men. They did rally, and came to the crest of the hill, when Colonel Stewart, Major Fraser, and Captain MacGregor, staff officers, and indeed every officer, with revolver and sword in hand, encouraged the men by word or action.

The whole Boer fire was turned on the last point of defence in the left rear. There the men were crowded behind a clump of stones, but the officers made them extend to the right and left, lest they should be outflanked. Our direct rear at one part was held by only thirty men; luckily, the ground there was so steep the Boers were unable to scale it, thus all their efforts were hurled against the left.

"Men of the 92nd Highlanders, don't forget your bayonets!" cried Major Fraser. Colonel Stewart called on the men of the 58th, and Captain MacGregor on those of the Naval Brigade, and all did their duty steadily and well.

In some places the Boers were seen, pipe in mouth, taking pot-shots quietly, as they do when practising at pumpkins rolling down a hill. Nearer and nearer the fatal cordon of death was closing round the devoted band on the hill of Majuba, and through the smoke the officers were seen doing their utmost to urge the defence. In the centre of a group that held a knoll was seen Sir George Colley, animating the men and behaving in the most resolute manner, though, one by one, they quickly dropped around him.

With fixed bayonets, and shoulder to shoulder, at last, formed in semicircle, our men continued firing, while ammunition began to fail Many more fell, but there was no shelter to which they could be removed, and, if there had been, not a man could have been spared to succour them.

The Boers at last reached the few men who held the true front; the latter brought their bayonets to the charge, but beyond striking distance, and all save three were shot down where they stood. With the general there were barely 100 men of the main body left. The advanced line had been long since shot down or driven in upon the last or main position. This has been described as being about 200 yards long by 50 broad, where the whole survivors now lined the rim of the basin with fixed bayonets to repel the assailants. The Boers, with fierce and exultant shouts, swarmed up the side of the hill, and made furious attempts to carry it at a rush, but each time were driven back by the bayonets, many of which were dyed with blood. After each rush the firing, which ceased during the *mêlée* broke out with renewed fury, and again the air became alive with whistling bullets.

All at once Sir George Colley was seen to throw his arms above his head, to reel wildly forward, and fall dead, shot through the brain, and then all was lost!

The *Daily Telegraph* asserted that he was shot in the act of giving the order to "cease firing," believing that all was over.

Gathering near the edge of the slope at that moment, the Boers made a headlong rush at a point beyond that which they had been before attacking, and where there were but few to oppose them. Like a living tide they burst over the edge, and the position was taken. The main line of the defenders—if such a term can be applied to the miserable remnant that remained—finding themselves taken in reverse, made a rush along the plateau and sought to rally, but in vain. The fierce shouts and storm of bullets came together. There was a mad rush with the Boers close behind; an eyewitness writes:

> The roar of musketry, the whistling of bullets, and the yells of the enemy made up a medley which seemed infernal. All around the men were falling; there was no resistance, no halt— it was a flight for life. At this moment I was knocked down by the rush and trampled upon, and when I came to my senses the Boers were firing over me at the retreating troops, who were moving down the hill I was taken prisoner, and led away. On the hill I found the body of Sir George Colley, shot through the head.

The *Times* says:

> The handful of Highlanders were the last to leave the hill, and remained there throwing down stones on the Boers, and receiving them at the point of the bayonet.

The 60th Rifles fought their way gallantly back to camp, and all their officers escaped.

Pell-mell down the slopes fled those who survived the defence of the hill, flying as British soldiers had never, perhaps, been seen to fly before, while the bullets hissed and tore after them. Tumbling over rocks and boulders, plunging down the rough *dongas*, a few got through the leaden storm and escaped; while others, worn by the weary night march, the dreadful ascent of the hill, and the horrors of a day of toil and slaughter, dropped exhausted, and were killed without resistance on their part, or compunction on that of the Boers, whose pursuit was checked when the camp guns were turned on them from Mount Prospect, and did considerable execution among them. No fears were entertained for the safety of the camp, but every preparation for a vigorous defence in case of an attack was made by Sir George Colley's successor in the command, Colonel Dunn Bond, of the 58th.

Tidings of the defeat excited great consternation at Pietermaritzburg and at Durban, where all the ships in harbour hoisted their colours half-mast high.

Several men who had concealed themselves in the rocky holes and jungle of the mountain, came dropping into camp by twos and threes next morning, worn out with fatigue and thirst. All night the rain fell heavily; the cold was intense. Some of the wounded men were carried to a farmhouse near the hill; but the majority lay where they fell, exposed to the inclemency of the weather, and many who fell into the *dongas* were never seen again.

None of the 60th Rifles were engaged in the defence of the position. General Wood telegraphed thus to Mr. Childers from Fort Amiel, on the 20th April, about the 60th:—

> None on Majuba. One company sent out with spare ammunition to join the supporting company of the 92nd, and retired with it by orders from Prospect Camp, bringing all the ammunition in. Two companies posted three miles off covered the retreat steadily, and I am perfectly satisfied with their behaviour.

It was computed that of the men who remained on the hill until the last of the conflict, not more than one in four escaped. "Only eighteen out of one hundred and twenty Highlanders returned to camp," according to the *Standard*; 180 are given as having been detailed. This telegram must have been an exaggeration or mistake. An Irishman named Aylward was at this time acting as military secretary to Commandant-General Joubert.

On hearing of General Colley's fall, Colonel Bond, of the 58th, commanding in the camp at Mount Prospect, while taking precautions for the defence of the latter, made arrangements to bring in the dead and wounded. Ambulance waggons, with flags of truce flying, were sent out with strong fatigue parties, amounting to 100 men, in charge of Dr. Howard Babbington and his staff.

The Boer general gave the *Times* correspondent a pass to the camp, on condition that he would show him his account of the engagement before despatching it to that journal, and inquired of him who was the officer of rank that had been killed. The reply was:

> 'Take me to him.' We went to where the body lay, with the face covered by the helmet. By the clothing I recognised the body, and, lifting the helmet, saw the face of our poor general, the bravest soldier of the day, a commander loved and admired by every man, from the highest to the lowest. The Boers doubted me, and questioned me again and again as to whether it was

really the general, I gave them my word of honour that it was really General Colley, and they were satisfied. No word of exultation escaped their lips. I said, 'You have killed the bravest gentleman in the field.' They said, 'Yes, he fought well.'

After the action the Boers were heard shouting to our men to come, as no harm would be done to them. Those who obeyed the summons were the only prisoners they made, as few were captured on the hill itself. Colonel Bond sent a note to the Boer *commandant*, asking him to restore the general's body, which was brought into camp in the afternoon, and lay for a considerable time in an ambulance waggon, near the hospital, attended by an orderly. There was one bullet-wound in the forehead; all the buttons had been cut off the uniform, as mementoes of the slain, probably.

It is said that when the party of red-coats bore the body out of the Boers' camp the commander of the latter sent a message of condolence to Lady Colley. The funeral took place at sunset. The body was conveyed to the grave on a gun-carriage. The pall-bearers were Colonels Ashburnham, Parker, and Bond; Majors Ogilvie and Elmes; Captains Vibart and Smith, with Lieutenant Brotherton.

Sir George Colley's widow was Edith Althea, daughter of Major-General Hamilton, C.B., Assistant Quartermaster-General in the Crimea. They were married in 1878. Another gallant officer was laid by his side, in presence of all the officers, and detachments from every regiment—Commander Romilly, who led the Naval Brigade.

Many who were marked as "missing" in the first casualty lists were afterwards found dead or wounded in the *dongas*, or among the jungle.

The Victoria Cross was bestowed upon Lance-Corporal Joseph John Farmer, of the Army Hospital Corps, for conspicuous and devoted bravery at Majuba. The *Gazette* says:

Where he showed a spirit of self-abnegation, and an example of cool courage which cannot be too highly commended. While the Boers closed with the British troops near the well, Corporal Farmer held a white flag over the wounded, and when the arm holding the flag was shot through, he called out that he had another. He then raised the flag with the other arm, and continued to do so until that also was pierced by a bullet.

The actual strength of the force engaged on and about Majuba Hill on the 27th amounted to thirty-five officers and 693 non-commissioned officers and men all told.

CHAPTER 14

The Battle of Tel-El-Kebir: 1882

The Battle of Tel-el-Kebir stands out pre-eminently as one of the most glorious achievements in the history of that gallant old regiment, the 79th Highlanders. The circumstances leading up to the battle were of a somewhat peculiar nature, and, briefly, are as follows. On the 26th June, 1879, the Khedive Ishmail, who had caused Britain much trouble, was ordered by the Sultan of Turkey to resign, and his son Tewfik was appointed as successor. A short period after this, Britain and France re-established dual control of Egypt, and this continued for two years.

About the end of that period a *fellah* officer, calling himself Ahmed Arabi, who had assisted Ishmail during his efforts to overthrow the constitutional ministry, headed a band of Arab officers, who complained of the preference shown to officers of Turkish origin. The dispute thereafter expanded into an attack on the privileged position of foreigners, and finally it was directed against all Christians, foreign and native.

The government was then too weak to suppress the disorder, and for the time being certain concessions were made to Arabi. That individual, from being made Under Secretary for War, was afterwards appointed to the Cabinet. But the danger of a serious rising brought the British and French Fleets, in May, 1882, to Alexandria, and after a massacre had been perpetrated by the Arab mob in that city on the 16th June, the British admiral bombarded the place.

The leaders of the national movement prepared to resist further British aggression by force. A conference of ambassadors was held at Constantinople. The *sultan*, on being invited to quell the revolt, hesitated, and the British Government determined to commence the work. France, invited to take part, declined, and Italy took up a similar attitude. It was thus that the Battle of Tel-el-Kebir came to be fought.

An expeditionary force, detailed from home stations and from Malta, was organised in two divisions, with a cavalry division, corps troops, and a siege train, numbering in all about 25,000 men. An Indian contingent, 7,000 strong, complete in all arms, and with its own transport, was prepared for despatch to Suez. General Sir Garnet Wolseley was in command, with Lieutenant-General Sir John Adye as chief of staff.

The camp of the enemy was situated on the southern slope of a ridge at Tel-el-Kebir, and was hidden by the folds of a plateau which lay between this and the British camp. Their lines were drawn from a canal on the south to the northern slopes of the ridge, the highest part of which was occupied by three works for their heavier artillery. It was evident that they dreaded a turning movement on one or both flanks. A part of the lines had been executed nearly a year before the war broke out, for Tel-el-Kebir was held by Egyptian (or rather by American) strategists to be a position of the greatest importance.

A single line of continuous trench, to which the Egyptians trusted, was prolonged northwards shortly before the battle, and the work was here only partly complete. Continuous lines are condemned by European military writers us essentially weak, because once broken at any point they are probably lost to their entire extent. Tel-el-Kebir was to prove the truth of this tactical axiom.

One open work for guns was erected on the south slope of the desert ridge. The soil being light, cover was easily obtained. The trenches were about deep enough to allow of a man firing easily over the parapet, and an exterior ditch, some four feet deep, was dug at most parts of the line outside the mound. The gun positions, which were conspicuous above the surface, had embrasures very neatly riveted with maize-sticks and mud, but in so dry and sandy a country they would probably have been much damaged by any heavy practice from the guns which they contained. Arabi Pasha had paid special attention to his flanks, and on the north a line of parapet ran almost south-west at an acute angle to the front, along the crest of the ridge, to defend the position from the much-dreaded turning movement on his left flank. The southern flank was protected by the canal, and the Wady, a river which Arabi intended to flood. A battery of four Krupp guns was here placed outside the canal.

Such was the position on which the Egyptian War Minister staked the fate of his army for the Tel-el-Kebir fight, having with him there some 26,000 men of his entire available army. About half of these, including some 6,000 negroes, the best troops to be found in Egypt, were trained soldiers, the rest being recruits of one or two months' standing, sent down in trains from the depot near Cairo, and drilled at first with clubs, until they were able to handle a rifle. In addition to his regular troops and recruits; Arabi had enlisted the services of some 6,000 Bedouin irregulars, both foot and mounted men. These were expected to make periodic raids on the British lines of communication.

These raids, however, were not carried out, for though the Bedouin *sheikhs* would ride furiously up and down in front of our outposts, as if to show their valour, a single shot was found sufficient to disperse them, and they refused to come nearer. Moreover, when one of them was wounded, the whole tribe followed him home in disgust. Thus, the Bedouin attacks were of little avail.

The British troops reached Kassassin, which is situated in the neighbourhood of Tel-el-Kebir, a few days before the battle was fought. The Bedouins, although they had not taken part in any fighting, hovered by night over the battlefield of Kassassin, where, a few days before, a vigorous attack by Arabi had failed. The Bedouins murdered or mutilated all the wounded who could not be shown to be Moslems.

While the Egyptian position covered the junction of the railways from Cairo and Belbeis, and was sufficiently strong, it had nevertheless its weak points, one of which was the intersected character of the country through which a retreat might have to be made. But the difficulty, which also of course affected the pursuit, would have arisen in almost any position taken up to oppose an advance from Ismaileh.

The line of operations chosen by the British general was incomparably the better of the two. The flat, open desert, without any natural features such as would interfere with evolutions on a large scale was far better suited for the advance than the narrow banks which lead from village to village at High Nile in the Delta itself. Thus, the advantage of taking the strong works of Keir-dowar in reverse, the shortening of the distance from Cairo, and the proximity of the important railway junction at Zaga-Zig were also considerations favouring the line adopted. The desert was generally hard enough for all arms, although some miles of drift sand had to be crossed.

To Arabi's forces may be added about sixty guns.

Against the forces mentioned above, the British mustered only 11,000 infantry, with 2,000 horse and 60 guns—a strength which, according to ordinary calculations, was quite unqualified for the task.

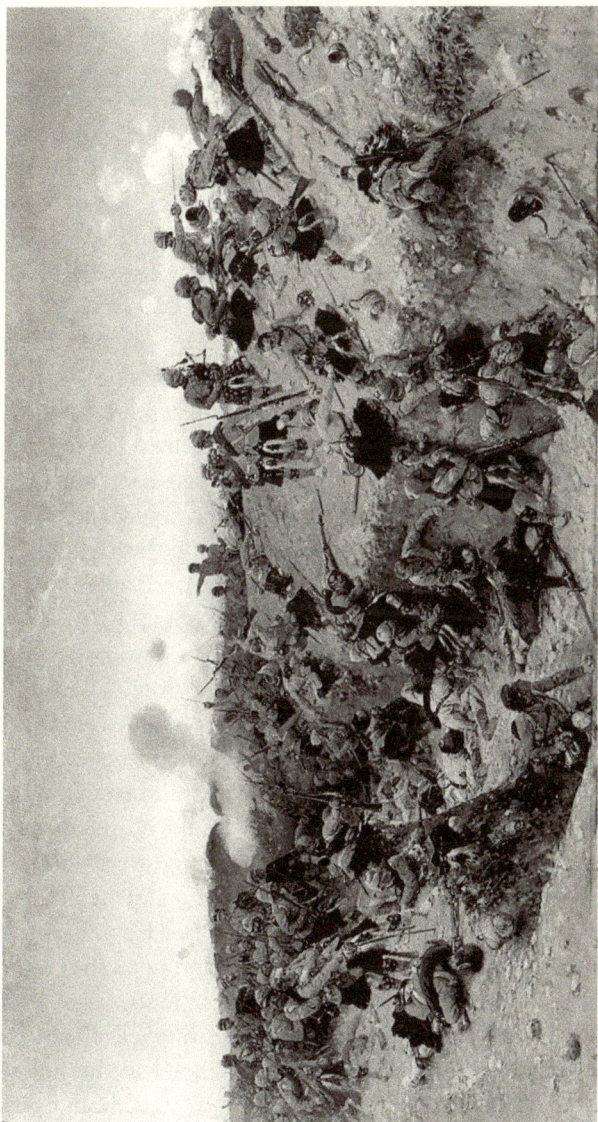

BATTLE OF TEL-EL-KEBIR

The British Army was extended into two lines, about a thousand yards apart, over a distance of three miles. The front line was composed of two brigades, whose duty it was to attack the highest part of the ridge—Graham's Brigade on the right and Alison's Highlanders on the left. Graham was supported by the guards, and between this and the supports of the Highland Brigade were 42 guns of the artillery division.

A gap of more than 2,000 yards was thus left between the Highlanders and the railway, along which the naval brigade and the ironclad train advanced. The Indian troops, who supported the Seaforth Highlanders, south of the canal, formed the extreme left of the British line. The cavalry division, held in reserve for pursuit, was on the extreme right in the second line. The reserve ammunition train, with the telegraph and pontoons, bringing up the rear.

The enemy were to be taken entirely by surprise, for Arabi had not been expecting the attack for a day or two yet, or from such a position, the British troops being stationed at Ismaileh. Notwithstanding this, when the great camp was struck at Kassassin at sunset, the news soon reached the enemy's ears, in spite of the secrecy maintained, and it is said that until midnight the Egyptians remained under arms, after which, in accordance with Oriental custom, they fell asleep, and, according to their own account, so remained until awakened by the shots of their outposts.

Sergeant Palmer, of the 79th Highlanders, in one of the most vivid published narratives of the battle, mentions that while the British Army lay camped at Kassassin the brigade orders issued on the morning of the 10th September, foreshadowed the night march on Tel-el-Kebir, which began the same evening. One of the instructions in those orders was that each man's water-bottle should be filled with cold tea—for the purpose, it is supposed, of keeping the soldiers awake. The regimental orders issued in the afternoon confirmed the brigade orders, and announced that the position of Tel-el-Kebir was to be attacked with the bayonet; no one was to load; and not a shot to be fired until the men were over the enemy's entrenchments.

The 79th, upon whom the bulk of the fighting fell, cheered vigorously when the orders were read to them. They had the fullest confidence in their leader, Sir Archibald Alison, who, although severe, is described as a just and reasonable man, well versed in war. There were thirteen victories inscribed upon the Highlanders' colours, but scarce a man in the rank and file had seen a battle, for it had been last in action during the Indian Mutiny.

The regiment paraded at 5.45 p.m. When the words "Stand at ease!" had been given, the captains of the respective companies explained to their men what they were to do to ensure victory at Tel-el-Kebir.

The remarks of Sergeant Palmer at this juncture are particularly impressive:—

Our captain was no great orator, but he had a straightforward, manly manner of speech, which somehow stirred the blood. As far as I can remember, this was what was said:—'Men, you are marching tonight to attack a strongly-entrenched position called Tel-el-Kebir, mounting some 60 guns, and sweeping our line of approach. On the march from Nine Gun Hill there must be no smoking. The strictest silence must be kept, and, unless ordered to the contrary, you are to continue the march steadily, no matter if bullets and shells come hailstone-fashion into the ranks. No bayonets are to be fixed till the order is given, and no man is to charge until the last note of the bugle is finished. The bayonet alone is to do the work, and not a shot is to be fired until the trenches are carried. You are to fight on so long as a man stands up. Remember the country and regiment to which you belong, and fight now as fought the Highlanders of old!'

It is further recorded that as the troops were marching to Nine Gun Hill chums were giving each other messages for home in case of being killed, for all knew there was hard fighting before them.

Reaching Nine Gun Hill, where lay their camp, the brigade in dense darkness deployed into line of half battalions of double companies at deploying intervals. During the halt at this hill, two lots of rum per man were served out—the first allowance of strong drink since quitting board ship. The regimental teetotaller called it "Dutch courage," but nobody needed an incentive to fight. The rum proved very comforting to the men in the chill night air, and when they had bolted it—for it had to be swallowed on the spot—most of them went to sleep; this to many their last sleep prior to the final long sleep of all. About 1.30 a.m. the march was resumed, the 79th being appointed the directing regiment, while Lieutenant Rawson, R.N., had the duty of guiding it by the stars.

Occasionally clouds would obscure the sky as the men plodded on, but the North Star and part of the Little Bear remained visible.

141

Sergeant Palmer and another non-commissioned officer were told off to march on the directing flank, close to Lieutenant Rawson. They were ordered to take off their helmets and keep their eyes fixed on a certain star, and if it should disappear, they were instructed to inform Rawson in a whisper. Within the space of one hour several stars disappeared, and as they did so the lieutenant indicated others for the men to watch. At this point the strictest discipline was maintained, and silence was vigorously enforced, save that occasionally a horse would neigh and another answer back in the cavalry ranks; not a sound was to be heard but the low trampling of many feet on the sand, described as resembling the fluttering of a flock of birds.

Once a man on whom either the rum had taken effect, or the weird silence had had an ungovernable influence, broke out into wild yells. Sir Garnet Wolseley immediately rode up, and ordered the offender to be bayoneted, but the regimental surgeon interposed, and begged leave to chloroform him instead. This was granted, and the man was drugged into insensibility and left lying on the sand.

After the troops had marched at a funeral pace for about two hours, a halt of twenty minutes was commanded. As the orders were slowly passed from company to company in a low tone of voice, they failed to reach the flanks of the brigade, which continued in motion, retaining the touch until the extremities all but met in front of the centre. Thus, the brigade in effect formed a great hollow circle. The line had to be laboriously straightened out and re-formed in the inky darkness, and in all but silence.

It was a fine proof of discipline that this was accomplished in the short space of twenty-five minutes, and about 4.30 a.m. the advance was resumed. Those present have described how the monotonous slow-step marching induced in them an almost overpowering sleepiness, somewhat incompatible, but not unusual, with a prospect of shortly facing the enemy.

The colonel of the 79th, Sir Archibald Alison, at this period was becoming anxious, and was beginning to fear that something was wrong, as the minutes slipped by and nothing was discovered of the enemy's position. Turning to Lieutenant Rawson, he exclaimed in a low tone, "Are we on the right track?"

"Yes, sir," was the reply; "we have the North Star on our right, and another in front, and soon we ought to be there."

Suddenly out of the darkness ahead appeared shadowy forms, an appearance followed up instantly by the crack of a rifle and the roar

142

of artillery. Never for a moment did the serried British ranks betray the confidence which had been placed in them, and though to spring forward was the impulse of every man, yet none stirred. Slowly and irresistibly the force moved forward. Here and there a man fell backward with a bullet through his head. The others made no sign.

All at once the order rang out sharp, "Fix bayonets!" and with alacrity the troops obeyed, the Highland regiments in the van. The order for the charge was now eagerly awaited, but the moment was not yet ripe.

For fully one hundred yards the silent force crept on, with arms at the slope, and the sound of the enemy's bullets upon the British bayonets has been likened to the sound of hailstones on a tin roof. Suddenly the welcome command, "Prepare to charge!" rang out on the early morning air, for dawn was breaking, and a sigh of relief went up from the eager troops. An, instant later and the "Charge!" was sounded. As the last note of the bugle died away, a mighty cheer went up, the pipes broke out into the slogan, and like a wave of the sea, with their gallant colonel at the head, shouting, "Come on, the Camerons!" the devoted Highlanders swept forward over the enemy's position.

A space of two hundred yards intervened before the first trench was reached, but at full speed, and shoulder to shoulder, not an instant was lost in traversing it. All the while the enemy fired vigorously, but fortunately aimed too high, and little damage was done. Now the charge was checked by the first trench, twelve feet in depth and twelve feet wide, which yawned in front of our men. Many fell headlong into it, but, scrambling and cheering, strenuously pushing, they gained the far side, and at length fell upon the enemy, steel to steel.

It is reported that the first man to gain the other side was a brave young soldier, Donald Cameron by name. He joined desperately hand to hand against a throng of Egyptians, till he received a bullet through the head and fell back bleeding into the trench, never to stir again. Others were by this time pushing forward, though the steepness of the trench proved an almost insurmountable obstacle. In spite, however, of constant slipping back, and the difficulty of obtaining foothold, soon large numbers of the Highlanders gained the summit of the trench, and, cleaving their way with the bayonet, they swept headlong on towards the second trench, with stentorian cheers. Here similar scenes were enacted, and many hand-to-hand conflicts took place ere the force halted for a moment and then resumed the victorious onslaught.

It is reported that between two trenches an extraordinary incident, and one which for a moment threatened to bring ruin to the British arms, occurred. Even as the Highlanders swept on towards the second trench there were loud shouts of "Retire! Retire!" and for an instant the ranks wavered. But not for long. Fortunately a staff officer in the nick of time galloped forward, and shouting, "No retire, men! Come on! come on!" led the hesitating ranks once more against the enemy.

Sergeant Palmer, to whose narrative we have before referred, gives the explanation of this singular occurrence, though the story is questioned by other writers. It seems that the cries of "Retire!" had been treacherously raised by a couple of Glasgow Irishmen, who had somehow evaded the precautions that were in force since the days of Fenianism to prevent the enlistment of disloyal characters. On two occasions they had been proved cowards, or something worse, and non-commissioned officers had been told off to watch their conduct in the field, it being left to the discretion of these to inflict summary justice if necessary. When the traitors were seen and heard to raise their coward voices, short shrift awaited them, and the bayonets of their fellows inflicted a speedy retribution.

In the rapidly-growing daylight it was now perceived that a short halt would be necessary to reform the somewhat scattered ranks, and this hastily effected, the brigade swept down before Tel-el-Kebir Lock, driving all opposition before them. Over the crest of the hill lay the white tents of the Egyptian camp, on the far side of the canal, and as the Highland ranks rushed on, the fugitive Egyptians threw themselves into the water in hundreds, and as many as gained the opposite bank were seen running like deer across the desert.

By now the 2nd Brigade arrived upon the scene, together with the Scottish division of the Royal Artillery at a gallop, and these quickly unlimbered and opened fire upon the rapidly-dispersing forces of Arabi. Then again dashing on, they took up a nearer position, and continued their deadly work. As they had passed the Highland Brigade a tremendous cheer went up from battery after battery, and loud shouts of "Scotland for Ever!" rent the startled desert air.

The Battle of Tel-el-Kebir was won. All that now remained was to push the victory, and this Sir Garnet was not long in doing. The 42nd were sent forward to clear the village, while the cavalry poured down across the desert in their hundreds. As these latter arrived, bitter disappointment was visible upon their faces, and they exclaimed as they shot past the now halted Highlanders in a whirl of dust, "You —— Jocks haven't left us the chance of a fight!" Such has ever been the spirit of the British soldier, and a brave show the cavalry made, as, with "flashing lances and waving swords," they swept on upon their work of annihilation.

The battle was won, but the casualty list was a heavy one, numbering 339 of all ranks. Of these no fewer than 243 occurred in the Highland Brigade, showing the lion's share which, that brigade had taken in the conflict.

Among the wounded lay the intrepid Lieutenant Rawson, through whose skilful leading the British plan of attack had met with so great success.

Says Sergeant Palmer:—

The sights of the battlefield were gruesome, now one looked at them in cold blood. The artillery had wrought fearful havoc. I remember one heap of twenty-four corpses, some blown absolutely into fragments, others headless and without limbs. In the outer trench our dead and wounded lay more thickly than those of the enemy, but in the inner trenches and in the spaces between, for one man of ours there were ten Egyptians.

Meanwhile, the British commander had prepared, with admirable foresight and patience, for the pushing home of his victory. The rapidity of the subsequent pursuit was even greater indication of sound military insight than the admirably-planned attack of the early morning. Cavalry and artillery vied with each other in cutting up and harassing the hard-pressed foe, now in full retreat at all points. For everywhere our arms had been successful.

The Indian contingent, moving out of camp at 2.30 a.m., having a shorter distance to cover than the main brigades, stormed the battery which defended the canal by attacking the gap which lay south of the Highlanders, and plied the defenders with canister at a range of 30 yards. There are few recorded instances in military history in which artillery have been so handled, fighting alone against infantry in an entrenchment, but the departure would appear to have been fully justified by events.

For already so shaken by the northern attack were the entrenched Egyptians, that they were quickly dispersed by the bold tactics of Colonel Schreiber's batteries, and a general rout ensued. By 4 p.m. on the same day, General Macpherson, with two squadrons of Indian horse, had reached Zag-a-zig, 26 miles distant, had captured the station, with five trains, and was in telegraphic communication with

Cairo. Fortunately, the orders issued by Arabi for the flooding of the district had not been carried out, or the position at Zag-a-zig would have been untenable.

The whole position was now in the hands of the British, and at length Arabi confessed himself beaten, surrendering "to that great nation, in whose clemency he placed his trust." Hereafter his army was entirely broken up, straggling along the canal to Zag-a-zig, where its disarmament took place. The enemy's rifles were either broken or thrown into the water.

The Egyptian dead numbered two thousand.

Not content, however, with the signal victory at Tel-el-Kebir, Sir Garnet Wolseley had more work to do, and a prompt dash on Cairo was no sooner conceived than carried into effect. Though it was well known that the city of Cairo was garrisoned by some 10,000 fresh troops and though the strength of its defences was admittedly formidable, Sir Garnet never hesitated for an instant.

By four o'clock in the afternoon of the 14th September, the day after the battle, the Indian cavalry brigade, with the 4th Dragoons and Mounted Infantry rode into the outskirts of Cairo, where the barracks were at once surrendered to them, some 50 troopers, a mere handful, accepting the submission of the garrison. Later the same evening another small detachment of 150 men demanded the submission of the citadel. So great was the prestige of our troops, that the 5,000 armed soldiers who formed the garrison inarched out submissively, and our Indian cavalry at once took possession, "riding like black demons into the formidable fortress."

On the 15th, Sir Garnet Wolseley, attended by the Foot Guards, and fresh from his victory at Tel-el-Kebir, arrived in Cairo by train, and the campaign was brought to a glorious and successful termination, barely three weeks from the time of landing the expeditionary force. Arabi himself was banished to Ceylon.

No praise can be too high for the secrecy and energy with which the enterprise was carried out, and all ranks came in for the hearty congratulations of the commander-in-chief. The Highland Brigade, upon whom fell the brunt of the work, justly recall Tel-el-Kebir as one of the most glorious of their many glorious victories.

CHAPTER 15

The Battle of Minhla: 1885

A period of comparative quiet prevailed in Burmah for some years following the conclusion of the war of '52. Gradually, however, this was broken, and on the accession of King Theebaw to the Burmese throne, in '78, relations between the Burmese and the Government of India became seriously strained. On his accession King Theebaw in the most cold-blooded manner massacred most of his nearest male relatives, and with these and other outrages it soon became undesirable to maintain a British convoy at the Court of Ava.

In 1879 this official was withdrawn from; Mandalay, and on his retirement, matters went from bad to worse. Ever intriguing, with first this Power and then that, it was felt that British prestige in Burmah was at a low ebb. Moreover, *dacoities* and persistent raiding by the hill-tribes served still further to unsettle the country, and so poor was the authority of the king that these lawless acts and expeditions threatened to overflow into British territory.

In the autumn of 1883, a particularly brutal and appalling massacre of 200 unarmed and defenceless prisoners in the Mandalay prison, by the orders of the king, still further augmented the trouble, and a considerable number of the subjects of the Burmese king crossed with their families into British territory, attracting the special attention of the Government of India to the prevailing state of affairs. Moreover, Bhamo, the second city of the kingdom of Burmah, had been captured by the Kachyin tribes, and these were expelled by the king only with the greatest difficulty—another evidence of Theebaw's incompetent ruling.

Two causes combined at this juncture to bring matters to a head. With a treasury impoverished by his expedition against the Kachyin's, Theebaw cast about him for a means of replenishing it, and his efforts to obtain a large loan from French sources was very closely watched

THE BATTLE OF MINHLA

by the Government of India, who naturally viewed the introduction of French capital with no very favourable eye. Unfortunately for Theebaw, his efforts to negotiate the French loan proved unavailing, and a convenient opportunity for repairing the deficiency presented itself in the alleged breach of contract on the part of the Bombay and Burmah Trading Company, which had worked the timber monopoly of the forests of Upper Burmah for the last few years. It was stated by the Mandalay authorities that the company's agents had been exporting, as subject to a low rate of duty, quantities of logs which were really of a description liable to pay a higher rate.

The first demand for back payment on this account was estimated at £100,000, which was £30,000 more than the company were owed by the king on account of previous advances made to him. The agents, however, declined to recognise the claim when it was first mooted in August, and the dispute was carried on till two months later, when a royal decree from King Theebaw put an end to the protests by awarding a fine of £230,000 against the company. This preposterous fine met with a remonstrance through the medium of the Chief Commissioner for British Burmah, and not only was this remonstrance unheeded, but in October the king's troops fired upon some of the Company's draughtsmen, bringing matters to a crisis.

Drastic action was the outcome of this unfortunate business—the immediate cause of the third Burmese war. The Viceroy of India issued an ultimatum to King Theebaw:—

> Requesting the latter to receive a British Resident at Mandalay, to settle the dispute in concert with the Burman Ministers, and asking for an explanation of the hostile conduct of the Burmese troops with regard to the company's servants.

The 10th November was fixed as a limit for the king's reply, and meantime a force was got together in preparation for eventualities, and the Burmese themselves prepared for the worst by massing their forces at Minhla on the Irrawaddy.

The time for parleying soon passed by without a satisfactory answer from King Theebaw, and on the 14th November the British expedition crossed the frontier.

Major-General, afterwards Sir, H. N. D. Prendergast, V.C., was placed in command, while Colonel Sladen accompanied the troops as chief political officer. A naval brigade, a field battery, two garrison batteries, one British, and two native mountain batteries, three European and seven native regiments of infantry, and six companies of sappers and miners made up the force. Brigadier-Generals Foord, White, V.C., and Norman commanded the first, second, and third brigades respectively, while Captain Woodward, R.N., was in charge of the naval detachment. The native troops hailed from Madras, Bengal, and Bombay, while the British regiments were composed of the Liverpool and Hampshire regiments of the 1st Battalion Royal Welsh Fusiliers. There were 10,000 men in all.

The part played by the naval brigade was of the utmost importance. The quickest and most satisfactory method of carrying out the campaign was at once seen to be an advance by water direct on the capital. At Rangoon were then lying a number of light-draught steamers belonging to the Irrawaddy Flotilla Company, and these with H.M.S. *Irrawaddy*, the armed launch *Kathleen* and other vessels made up the river transport and defence. No fewer than 55 steamers, barges, launches, etc., were employed in the advance. This began on the 14th November. One account says:—

> There is not the slightest doubt that the Burmese king and his country were taken completely by surprise by the unexampled rapidity of the advance.

A minor naval engagement was the opening one of the campaign. Moving out of Thayetmyo, the British post on the river nearest the frontier, the *Irrawaddy*, on the 14th, the first day of the advance, engaged the first Burmese batteries she came across, some 28 miles upstream, and was successful in cutting out the king's steamer and some barges, which she brought back in triumph and without a casualty to our arms. Two days later the batteries themselves were captured by a land force, after a very feeble show of resistance.

On the 17th, however, at Minhla, where indeed most resistance had been anticipated, the Burmese made a determined stand. Successively they held a barricade, a *pagoda*, and the palace and redoubt of Minhla. A somewhat simple plan of attack was decided upon, which proved highly successful. The forts were to be attacked from the land face by troops landed higher up the river, and marched down through the dense undergrowth, while the naval brigade was to feint a determined onslaught from the river or front of the position.

Seven miles below Minhla, on the morning of the 17th, the land forces were disembarked, the first and second brigades on the left bank, the third on the right, for the forts were on both sides of the river. Immediately after the landing, the Irrawaddy and Kathleen made all speed up stream to Minhla, and soon the terrific noise of their great guns told of the commencement of the feint attack. Slowly and stealthily the troops crept forward in the dense underbush. Presently Kolegone on the left bank, the strongest of the Minhla forts, was reached, and, to the surprise of all, it was found to be empty. Shaken by the gunboats, and learning at length of the advance of a great land force, the Burmese, leaving only a few wounded, had evacuated the fort.

But the fighting was to come. On the right bank the enemy held a strong barricade in front of Minhla, and an obstinate resistance had to be overcome with cold steel ere the foe was driven out. Lieutenant Drury was killed here, and other officers wounded, but the fighting was not for long. Driven out of their barricade into a *pagoda*, and from there again into Minhla itself, the harassed Burmese eventually became victims to a panic.

Throwing down their arms, others jumping in the river, many fleeing over land, the soldiers of King Theebaw fled in all directions, leaving 170 killed and nearly 300 prisoners in our hands. The British casualties totalled 36, of whom only five were killed, one being an officer. This, the most important engagement of the campaign, thus proved itself to be a victory cheaply bought, and in confidence and high spirits the troops moved out of Minhla on the 19th, leaving only a small garrison to hold the place against a possible recapture.

No further resistance, with the exception of a little desultory firing on the far side of Pagau, the ancient city of temples, was now met with for nearly a hundred miles up the river, but on the 24th of the month the fleet came in sight of Mingyan, where the whole Burmese Army was reported to be assembled. Here, as before, resistance was slight, the task of turning the enemy out of their position being entrusted to the naval guns. Though Mingyan was not reached until the evening, Captain Woodward at once opened a terrific fusillade, and soon silenced the enemy's batteries and musket fire, driving all before him. Darkness now put a stop to the operations, but on resuming firing in the morning it was found that the Burmese had cleared out with heavy loss. British casualties were virtually nil, two or three men only being slightly wounded.

The route to Mandalay now lay open, and news was apparently carried to King Theebaw of the irresistible British advance, for on the afternoon of the 26th, as the flotilla was approaching Ava, envoys from the king approached General Prendergast with offers of surrender.

The general's reply was brief and to the point—only in the capital could details of surrender be arranged. The steady forward movement was recommenced.

On the 28th of the month Mandalay was occupied without resistance, the city's defences being at once occupied by our soldiery.

Says a published record:—

> The people seemed everywhere of a friendly disposition, and the soldiery gave up their arms and were allowed to disperse, a measure which afterwards proved highly disquieting, though the consequences of it could not at the time have been foreseen. There was doubtless a considerable party in the capital favourable to the palace and its inmates, as could only be expected; so, after an interview with the king, and a slight survey of the state of affairs in Mandalay. Colonel Sladen advised General Prendergast to let Theebaw and his family be sent out of the city without delay, for fear of an outbreak of the plundering hangers-on of the late favourites.

Accordingly, on the 29th November, the obstinate Theebaw and his wives were despatched by river to Rangoon, an exit which marked the termination of the royal reigning dynasty in Burmah, for on January 1st, 1886, rather more than a month from the occupation of Mandalay, a Viceregal proclamation was promulgated through the late Burmese Empire. "One of the shortest documents of its kind," it ran as follows:—

> By command of the Queen Empress, it is hereby notified that the territories formerly governed by King Theebaw will no longer be under his rule, but have become part of Her Majesty's dominions, and will, during Her Majesty's pleasure, be administered by such officers as the Viceroy and Governor-General of India may from time to time appoint.

In such unmistakable and uncompromising terms was the annexation of Burmah accomplished.

Meanwhile, intriguers were found to be at work, and it was decided that the continued presence of King Theebaw, though a prisoner, was undesirable in Burmah. The king, quite a young man, was accordingly despatched to Madras, with a chosen band of attendants, where he was lodged, pending orders.

Fighting, however, was not yet entirely over, for almost immediately after the occupation of Mandalay and the disbandment of Theebaw's army, *dacoities* began to take place all over the country, especially in the immediate neighbourhood of the capital, from which it is surmised these attacks were organised and probably executed by gangs of the late soldiery. The Tinedah-Woon indeed, said to have been one of the chief instigators of the late king's warlike enterprises, was captured on the night of the 28th whilst attempting to leave the city disguised as a *coolie* or common; labourer.

But, however instigated, these *dacoities* proved a serious trouble and menace to British authority, and some stiff fighting, attended however with little loss of life, had to be gone through before the country was finally pacified.

An unfortunate incident which occurred is worthy of record, as it concerned the company so intimately connected with the above events. Seven European *employés* of the Bombay and Burmah Company were engaged in timber operations up the Chindwyin River, at Keedat, at the time the ultimatum was despatched to Mandalay, and three of them were killed during their attempt to obey the order to return, and the rest imprisoned for a time. They were only released by a timely and rapid march from the Manipuri State, headed by Colonel Johnstone, the political agent there, aided by Manipuri troops.

During the month of February, 1886, Upper and Lower Burmah were, under Mr. C. Bernard, as Chief Commissioner, united into one province. On the 31st March, General Prendergast left Mandalay on the successful termination of his mission.

CHAPTER 16

The Battle of the Atbara: 1898

The struggle for supremacy in Egypt was far from being finally settled at Tel-el-Kebir. With the voice of discontent, bursting now and again into open revolt, with that potent influence, fanaticism, always at work, small wonder that the Soudan was the scene of perpetual conflict, and at length matters reached a crisis at the end of 1897.

The voice of rumour, growing louder and ever nearer, at length brought warning to Sir Herbert Kitchener, the *Sirdar* of the Anglo-Egyptian Army, of threatening movements of a *dervish* force near Berber, and Anglo-Egyptian reinforcements were promptly hurried to the front to stem the tide of what promised to be a formidable revolt. The Egyptian Army was at this time in a very complete state of organisation, thanks to the great brain which day and night watched ever its growth and prepared it against all eventualities, and now the time had come for action the ultimate issue of events was confidently awaited in Britain.

General Sir Herbert Kitchener had had fifteen years' experience of Egypt. He had been Intelligence Officer in Sir Garnet Wolseley's campaign, commander at Suakim, fought with success again and again against Osman Digna, and finally succeeded Sir Francis Grenfell as Commander-in-chief in Egypt. No man was better acquainted with the Egyptian question, and none knew better how to meet the coming difficulty.

The *dervish* forces were under the leadership of Mahmud and Osman Digna, and were reported to be marching steadily northward, with an ever-growing army, to attack the British force.

That force was now rapidly set in motion. With such men as Kitchener, Hunter, Macdonald, and Gatacre, to name but a few, no loss of time or energy took place, and in a few short weeks a formidable British force, admirably equipped in all arms and perfectly organised, was marching southward.

By March 1, the reinforcements were at Berber, some 25 miles from the junction of the Nile and the Atbara Rivers, near which place it was rumoured that the *dervish* army, instead of advancing to the attack, were strongly entrenching themselves against our force. By this time the British Army in the field numbered some 12,000 to 13,000 men. They were divided into four brigades. Three of these were Egyptian, under the chief command of General Hunter. The fourth was British. The first brigade, under General Macdonald, comprised the 9th, 10th and 11th Soudanese, and the 2nd Egyptian, and it is not too much to say that never had any troops, British or native, more confidence in their sturdy leader.

General Macdonald had risen from the ranks, after conspicuous and repeated gallantry in Afghanistan. He had been taken prisoner in the Boer War at Majuba, and fought gallantly with his Soudanese at Gemaizeh, Tooki, and Afafit, and it is safe to say his devoted troops would have followed him wherever he might be pleased to lead them. These troops were at Berber. The second brigade, of similar constitution, three Soudanese regiments, the 12th, 13th, and 14th, together with the 8th Egyptian, was under the command of Colonel Maxwell, and quartered half way between Berber and Atbara, while at the latter place, and not far removed from the enemy's outposts, was the third, or Egyptian, brigade, under Colonel Lewis.

The total strength of the Egyptian Army was thus brought up to some 10,000 men, with 46 guns, while three gunboats operated on the Nile from Atbara. The fourth, or British, brigade, was under the charge of General Gatacre, and, after a forced and memorable march to Berber, in the first part of which the admirably constructed Egyptian railway played a valuable part, had encamped in the neighbourhood of the second brigade at Debeika. The Lincolnshire (10th), the Cameron Highlanders (79th), and the Warwickshire made up the force, while the 1st Seaforth Highlanders, under Colonel Murray, were daily expected. A maxim battery completed their equipment. Thus, the total force under the *sirdar's* supreme command may be estimated at 14,000 men, with 52 guns in all.

The precise strength of the enemy was unknown, but it has been variously estimated at 15,000 to 20,000. The Arab spy is notoriously indifferent to accuracy, and thus precise particulars were almost unobtainable, in spite of the most strenuous efforts of Colonel Wingate, the chief of our Intelligence Department.

CAMERON HIGHLANDERS TAKING THE STOCKADE

By the 16th March the whole Anglo-Egyptian force was concentrated at Kemir, some seven miles from Fort Atbara, and the men of all ranks and regiments, in the pink of condition, were keen and eager for the fight. Some days, however, were now spent in reconnoitring the enemy's position, and in this connection invaluable services were rendered by the gunboats which patrolled the river. Almost daily did these seek a brush with the enemy's outposts, and both loot and invaluable information were brought back to camp by the enterprising naval commanders.

Says the late G.W. Steevens, in his famous work on the campaign:—

You may imagine that the officers of Her Majesty's Navy did not confine their work to looking on. A day or two ago, Mahmud had been transferring his war material in barges from Metemmeh to Shendi (a point some hundred miles up the Nile). Knowing the ways of 'the devils,' as they amiably call the gunboats, he had entrenched a couple of hundred riflemen to cover the crossing. But one gunboat steamed cheerfully up to the bank and turned on the maxims, while the other sunk one 'nuggar' and captured two.

With minor engagements of this nature, and in the camp hard drill and busy preparation, the days passed by, till at length, on the morning of Sunday, March 20th, the force moved out of Kemir, southwards, in the direction from which the enemy were known to be advancing. Two days previously the long-expected Seaforths had arrived in camp, and met with a warm reception from their British and Egyptian comrades!. They arrived "smiling all over, from colonel to private, to find they were in time."

Great was the joy of all ranks when it was at length announced that Mahmud's force was on the Atbara River, and almost certain to give battle. Rumours were rife at this time, the most credible being that Mahmud had seized the Hudi ford, a few miles south of Fort Atbara, but on reaching here on March 20th and 21st, not a dervish was to be seen. The same day, however, as Hudi was reached, the cavalry had a brush with a party of advanced dervish horse, and succeeded in chasing them off into the bush. Our men, however, lost seven troopers killed, the first casualties of the campaign.

By this time the sand and dust of the desert had been exchanged for the thickly-grown, low-lying land of the Atbara, and the change was a welcome one in many ways, though indeed the scrub afforded ample cover for the enemy. The day following this a stronger reconnoitring force encountered some more *dervish* cavalry, and shots were exchanged, which brought the whole army to the front hot foot, but with the emptying of a few *dervish* saddles the incident terminated. Everything, however, tended to show that a general engagement could not be long delayed. And for our officers and men, the sooner it came the better, for though food was plentiful, the camp equipments were scanty, and comfort almost unknown.

Says Mr. Steevens at this stage:—

Though the Soudan can be live coals by day, it can be aching ice by night. Officers and men came alike with one blanket and no overcoat, for you must remember that we left Kemir with the intention of fighting: the next day or the next.

The Egyptian Army were better off than their British comrades. Knowing the Soudan, an Egyptian officer summed up the difference of the equipments of the two armies in a single sentence:—

I've been in this country five years, so when I was told to bring two days' kit, I brought a fortnight's.

The British, however, unprepared for the long delay, had to make the best of things, and those discomforts, added to the eagerness of the men, made a general engagement the one prayer of all. On the 27th March, Haig's reconnaissance of the Atbara River took place, but for a distance of 18 miles not a sign of Mahmud was to be seen, only "the impenetrable, flesh-tearing jungle of mimosa spears and half a grass, through which no army in the world could possibly attack."

On the morning of the 27th, the 15th Egyptian, with some friendly Yadin, who had many old scores to settle with Mahmud, arrived at Shendi in three gunboats, and, surprising a large party of the enemy, captured nearly 700 prisoners, mostly women, and killed 160 of the Baggara warriors. The captives were brought down to Fort Atbara, where they "are now probably the wives of such black soldiers as are allowed to marry."

This important encounter, the result of the *sirdar's* carefully laid plans, almost certainly forced the engagement. For, distressed at the loss of their women, and now unable to retreat to Shendi, the fighting men of Mahmud's army must be distracted at all costs. A fight with the British must occur without delay if the *khalifa's* enterprise is to succeed As yet the precise position of the enemy's main force was unknown, but at last, on March 30th, General Hunter's reconnaissance located them, and the joyful news went round the camp like wildfire.

Nakheila, 18 miles away, on the Atbara, formed the stronghold of Mahmud. The general "had gone on until he came to it," says Steevens:—

> He had ridden up to within 300 yards of it and looked in. The position faced the open desert, and went right back through the scrub to the river. Round it ran a tremendous *zareba*.

For a few days speculation was rife in camp as to the next move. Here was the enemy at last, note attacking as expected, but waiting to be driven from his entrenched position either by bayonet or hunger. What means would be adopted to accomplish a successful issue?

The decision was not long in coming. By April 3rd, the camp was at Abadar, on the 5th at Umdabieh—nearer, ever nearer to the enemy. A brush here and there was of daily occurrence now, and raiding became part of the routine. The description by Mr. Steevens of the scene of one such raid gives a vivid picture of the state of affairs at this juncture.

He was returning with the camel corps convoy from Fort Atbara, whither during the days of waiting they had ridden for supplies, when:—

> Suddenly one of the men discerned cases lying opened on the sand about a hundred yards off the trampled road. Anything for an incident. We rode listlessly up and looked. A couple of broken packing-cases, two tins of sardines, a tin of biscuits half empty, a small case of empty soda bottles with *sirdar* stencilled on it, and a couple of empty bottles of whisky. Among them lay a cigarette box, a needle and reel of cotton, and a badge— A.S.C.—such as the Army Service Corps wear on their shoulder-straps. We were on the scene of last evening's raid. Two camels, we remembered, had been cut off and their loads lost.

With such incidents as these, and another reconnaissance in force by Hunter, terminating in a miniature battle with seventeen casualties, the evening of the 7th April arrived. In the early morning of the 8th, Good Friday, the long-expected battle was to be fought.

Dawn was the hour fixed for the attack. Unlike the approach to Tel-el-Kebir, the night of the march immediately preceding the battle on the Atbara was conspicuous for its brilliant moonlight. At six the force moved out of Umdabieh. At seven a halt was called, and till nearly one o'clock the troops rested. Some ate, some slept, but all were at last assured of the certainty of the morrow's action.

At one o'clock the march was resumed, and, under the guidance of Bunbashi Fitton of the Egyptian Army, the *dervish zareba* was cautiously, but surely, approached by the Anglo-Egyptian squares. Between four and five another halt took place, and the prospective battle was discussed in low tones in the prevailing cold. Some slept once more, others shivered, waiting for the dawn. At length the sun rose and disclosed the enemy's position right in front and the serried ranks of Britain ready to give battle.

Says Mr. Steevens:—

The word came, and the men sprang up. The squares shifted into the fighting formations, and at one impulse, in one superb sweep, nearly 12,000 men moved forward towards the enemy. . . .The awful war machine went forward into action.

Twenty-four guns, under Colonel Long, were on the right flank, and 12 maxims were divided among the right and left flanks and the centre. Crash! broke out the roar of artillery, and in an instant the front of Mahmud's camp was raked from end to end. The puffs of smoke floated lazily across the foreground as the iron hail tore its way into the quick-set hedge of the *zareba*, and here and there flames sprang out where the rockets compassed their work of relentless destruction. Once during the awful cannonade, the *dervish* cavalry formed up on the extreme left of the position, emerging from the bush in handfuls, but a heavy maxim fire soon drove them back.

For fully half an hour the enemy made no reply, and then, after this interval, the bullets began to whistle over the heads of the Anglo-Egyptian force. As at Tel-el-Kebir, the fire of the *dervishes* was aimed too high, and little damage was done.

At 7.30 the "Cease Fire!" sounded, and the infantry moved forward to the attack. The commanding officers of the various regiments made stirring speeches to their men. Colonel Murray, addressing the Seaforth Highlanders, said:—

The news of victory must be in London tonight.

General Gatacre's words were to the point, "there was to be no question, about this, they were to go right through the *zareba* and drive the *dervishes* into the river." The moment had arrived. The bu-

160

gles sounded the "Advance!" the pipes screamed out "The March of the Cameron Men" with that voice of glorious memories and lust for battle which the pipes convey when heard in war, and the force swept forward on the foe.

Upon the Cameron fell a prominent part. They were to clear the front with a hot rifle fire, and while some were doing this, others were to tear opens in the *zareba* or surmount it by scaling ladders. Next behind them followed the Lincolns, the Seaforths, and the Warwickshires. For a few moments as the force rushed forward, the enemy made never a sound. Then suddenly, as the Cameron reached the crest of the ridge overlooking the *zareba*, the murderous fire broke out.

Fortunately, as always in the Soudanese campaigns, the fire was for a great part too high, and the casualties, though heavy, were not so great as might have been expected. Meanwhile, General Macdonald's brigade advanced, and only about a minute elapsed from the time the combined force crowned the rise of the hill till the Cameron and Soudanese had torn down the *zareba* and made way for the main body of the army.

An eye-witness says:—

General Gatacre, accompanied by Private Cross, was actually the first, at the *zareba*. Cross, of the Cameron, bayoneted a big *dervish* who was aiming point blank at the general.

The simultaneous right attack by the Egyptians and Soudanese was also a fine spectacle. General Hunter himself, helmet in hand, led his men on to the *zareba*, but thirty yards from it was a strong stockade, backed by entrenchments, and this too had to be stormed. It was a thrilling quarter of an hour, and nothing could be finer than the way these almost insurmountable obstacles were tackled by our troops, and that in the face of the hottest, fire imaginable from the *dervish* defenders.

Inside the *zareba*, from behind stockades, and from holes in the ground swarmed the black, half-naked *dervishes*, running everywhere, turning now and again to fire at their assailants, but making ever for the river. Scores of them, lay stretched upon, the ground. The slaughter was awful. Gradually the ground grew clearer. The maxims had galloped right up to the stockade and poured their merciless fire into the living contents of the *zareba*. The Warwicks "were volleying off the blacks as your beard comes off under a keen razor." Death and destruction reigned on every side.

But the British had lost heavily. Captains Findlay and Urquhart of the Camerons had been killed storming the *zareba*. Lieutenant Gore of the Seaforths fell in the same place, and, indeed, most of our casualties were sustained at this place. "Never mind me, lads; go on!" called Captain Urquhart as he fell stricken; and go on they did, killing and slaying at every step. Piper Stewart of the Camerons was killed leading the way.

The fight was now practically over. Only the pursuit remained. On stumbled our men over the broken ground. Till Mr. Steevens says:—

Suddenly there came a clear drop underfoot—the river. And across the trickle of water the quarter mile of dry sandbed was a flypaper with scrambling spots of black. The pursuers thronged the bank in double line, and in two minutes the paper was still black spotted, only the spots scrambled no more.

"Now that," panted the most pessimistic senior captain in the brigade, "now I call that a very good fight!" Shortly after this the "Cease Fire!" sounded, and only the cavalry pursuit remained.

Nearly 4,000 prisoners had been taken, including Mahmud himself, who was found hiding beneath a native litter. Zeki, formerly Governor of Berber, was killed. Osmani Digna, wily to the last, had again escaped, but all the other important *dervish emirs* were among the dead. The former, with his horsemen, at an early period of the action got into the river bed and made off in the direction of Damara. They were pursued by General Lewis's cavalry, but the jungle on the river banks was so dense that the pursuit had to be abandoned. Colonel Broadwood, however, chased a large party of *dervishes* into the desert, where he captured a number of prisoners.

The British casualties were three officers and 18 men killed, with 88 wounded. Four British officers and two British non-commissioned officers belonging to the Egyptian and Soudanese brigades, and 14 native officers were wounded, while the native regiments lost 50 killed and 319 wounded.

Other accounts put the total Anglo-Egyptian loss at 81 killed and 493 wounded, out of the 12,000 men in action. The *dervish* dead alone numbered 3,000, and Mahmud's ten guns and hordes of prisoners showed the significance of the crushing victory at the Atbara. The jubilation among the British force was great, and loud cheers marked the termination of the battle. After the engagement, the *sirdar*, who had been under fire all the morning, rode over the battlefield. He was received with enthusiastic cheers by every regiment of the British brigade, which he thanked individually for their gallant victory. He also received an ovation from the Egyptian and Soudanese, among whose trophies were a great number of standards, spears, and drums, in recognition of the signal gallantry shown by the native troops.

The *sirdar* provisionally promoted on the field a sergeant-major of each native battalion which crossed the *zareba*, to subaltern rank. In conversation with Colonel Money, whose helmet had been traversed by a bullet, the *sirdar*, referring to the slow and steady advance of the Camerons under a withering fire when attacking the *zareba*, said:—

> It was one of the finest feats performed for many years. You ought to be proud of such a regiment."

Colonel Money replied that he was "right proud of it."

In the afternoon the three British officers killed and the 18 British soldiers who fell in the action were buried on the gravelly slope near the *zareba* where they met their fate, and the graves were afterwards covered with a *zareba* to prevent their desecration. An eye-witness says:—

> The burial service was most impressive. It was attended by the *sirdar*, Generals Hunter and Gatacre and their respective staffs, by every officer off duty, and by detachments of all the regiments. No farewell shots were fired, but a firing party presented arms, and the band of the 11th Soudanese and the Highland pipers played laments.

Inside the *zareba*, visited after the fight, the *dervishes* lay dead in scores, choking the rifle pits and entrenchments. One who was present at this exploration of the late battlefield says:—

> It was curious to see the Soudanese soldiers filling their water-bottles from a pool containing dead *dervishes*.

About an hour after sunset, the wearied troops returned to their camp at Umbadieh, which they reached about three o'clock on the Saturday morning. The wounded started an hour or two later.

The captive Mahmud attracted much attention, and all were eager to catch a glimpse of the famous Arab leader. To the *sirdar*, who interviewed him, he said little but that the campaign had been conducted at the *khalifa's* orders. He preserved a stoical silence on all other subjects, and seemed indifferent as to his fate. He was described by those

163

who saw him as a remarkable-looking man, of grand physique and good features. One of these says:—

> He has a dignified presence, and a quite natural haughty disregard of the common herd. He looks intelligent and strong-willed. He is being well treated. In his captured stronghold were found six heads fixed on poles, and one body, dreadfully mutilated.

On the Sunday following the battle, when the camp had been moved from Umbadieh to Abadar, a great church parade was held, and a thanksgiving service for victory conducted by the chaplains of all denominations present with the forces. At its conclusion the British Brigade was formed up in square, and the *sirdar*, advancing to the centre, read a telegram from the queen, which filled the heart of every listener with pride, greatly rejoice," said Her Majesty, "at brilliant victory." And then, with her infallible consideration and womanly sympathy, "I desire to be fully informed as to the state of the wounded."

Needless to say, the reading of this message provoked the wildest enthusiasm, and at the call of the *sirdar* three hearty cheers for the queen rent the stifling desert air. Other congratulations were to follow. From the *khedive*, Mr. Balfour on behalf of the government, Lord Lansdowne, Lord Cromer, and others too numerous to mention heartfelt expressions of joy and pride kept pouring in, the *sirdar*, in conclusion said:—

> In short, everyone is extremely proud of the conduct of the army in the field.

It is impossible to take leave of the Battle of the Atbara without quoting somewhat extensively from the narrative of a soldier who was through the fight. Corporal Inglis, of the Cameron Highlanders, gives a vivid picture of the great engagement, this gallant non-commissioned officer writes:—

> As we approached the enemy's position, my feelings got a bit of a shock. I was thinking of home, and wondering if that day was to finish my existence, when a large flock of vultures came swooping down, and settled right in front of us. I had often read about them, but never saw them before. Some instinct surely tells them of a coming battle. It made a lot of our fellows feel queer for a bit, as the big brutes kept walking up and down, looking at us. We moved on till within 500 yards of the enemy's

front. We could see all was bustle and excitement within the camp. We halted, charged magazines with several rounds, and sat down with fixed bayonets, and for the next hour were interested spectators of the Egyptian artillery shelling the enemy. . . . Just as the advance sounded, one of our men was shot through the head.

We ran under a heavy fire till within one hundred yards of the *zareba*, when we got on the knee and poured in five terrible volleys. What a terrific noise! We could see the enemy looking over their *zareba* and laughing in our faces, all the while keeping up a heavy fire upon us. We ran till close to the *zareba*. I was in the front rank, and another chap and I caught hold of a branch, and, turning, hauled it clean away, leaving the palms of our hands badly torn and bleeding. Men at other parts did the same, and as soon as the *dervishes* saw their protection giving way, they jumped out of the pits (in which they were lying), fired a volley into our midst, and eventually turned tail. Clutching my rifle in my hand, the fearful work now began of bayoneting the *dervishes* in the pits. Lots of them could not got out, and they fought in desperate fashion,

The treachery of the *dervishes* is well shown by the same graphic narrator:

One lance-corporal was running up the hill through their huts when three of them made for him. He shot one, bayoneted another, and then the third man threw down his spear and held up his hands (in token; of surrender). The lad pointed to the rear, allowing his captive the way to take for safety, and was in the act of running after the enemy again, when the man he had spared picked up a rifle and blew the lance-corporal's brains out. General Gatacre was running up behind, and, seeing the incident, gave the *dervish* such a blow with his sword that he nearly severed his head from his body. After that the order was given to show no mercy. It was not easy to distinguish the men from the women. A woman was on the point of being stabbed, when the fellow discovered his mistake and, laughing, turned away, when she immediately ran a spear clean through him. In an instant four bayonets pierced her body. On ceasing fire, I found myself alone, wondering how I had escaped, and a fervent 'thank God!' escaped my lips.

With such stirring tales as this the Battle of the Atbara waft brought to a successful issue, and crushing was its effect upon the forces of the *khalifa*. Not until September were the *dervish* forces able once more to confront the arms of Britain, and then for the last time.

CHAPTER 17

The Battle of Omdurman: 1898

Though the snake of *Mahdism* had been severely scotched at the Atbara, it was far from being killed, and from the termination of that battle preparations were steadily pushed forward for the final overthrow of the *khalifa*.

The magnitude of these preparations was upon a scale never before seen in, the Soudan, and the army, assembled at Wad Hamed by the end of August, the largest that had ever taken the field in that disordered region. Regiment by regiment the troops poured into the town of Wad Hamed, the point of concentration chosen by the *sirdar*, till the Egyptian Army had been raised to nearly double its strength, and its attendant flotilla of gunboats vastly augmented. The railway had been pushed forward to Atbara, and, trainload after trainload, the troops dismounted almost upon the scene of the former battlefield, and pushed steadily southward, British, Egyptian, and even the recent *dervish* foe, all pressed into the service of the British Army.

Mr. Steevens' description of the changed conditions at Atbara is graphic in the extreme:—

The platform was black and brown, blue and white, with a great crowd of natives. For drawn up in line opposite the waiting trucks were rigid squads of black figures. The last time we had seen, these particular blacks they were shooting at us. Every one had begun life as a *dervish*, and had been taken prisoner at or after the Atbara. Now, not four months after, here they were, erect and soldierly, on their way to fight their former masters, and very glad to do it. . . . . In mid-April the Atbara was the as yet unattained objective of the railway; in mid-July the railway was ancient history, and the Atbara was the point of departure for the boats. Just a half-way house on the road to Khartoum.

And, adds Mr. Steevens sententiously, "What a man the *sirdar* is!" Indeed, such organisation has seldom been, seen before or since.

The force destined to overthrow the last stronghold of *Mahdism* was made up of two infantry divisions, one British and one Egyptian; one British cavalry regiment, and ten squadrons of Egyptian horse, and eight companies of camel corps, with batteries of artillery, a siege train; and maxim the latter to be used with deadly effect against the army of the *khalifa*. The usual medical services and transport, both by land and river, completed the equipment. Six "fighting gunboats" accompanied the expedition.

The British infantry division was under the command of Major-General Gatacre, and Colonels Wauchope and Lyttelton respectively commanded its two brigades. The first brigade was made up to nearly 3500 strong, and consisted of Camerons, Seaforths, Lincolns, and Warwicks, with a maxim battery. Four battalions, each over 1,000 strong, of respectively 1st Northumberland Fusiliers, 2nd Lancashire Fusiliers, 2nd Rifle Brigade, and the 1st Grenadier Guards constituted the second brigade. The whole division was thus about 7,500 strong.

The Egyptian Infantry division consisted of four brigades (in place of the three which had fought at the Atbara), and its first, second and third brigades respectively under the commands of Macdonald, Maxwell, and Lewis, were constituted as before. The fourth, under Collinson Bey, consisted of the 1st, 5th, 17th, and 18th Egyptian regiments. The total Egyptian Division numbered 12,000 men.

The cavalry numbered 1,500 in all, of whom 500 were the 21st Lancers, under Colonel Martin, and the remainder Broadwood Bey's Egyptian horse. Long Bey, of the Egyptian Army, had supreme command of the artillery—forty-four guns and twenty maxims.

With camel corps and transport, the total land force numbered some 22,000 men of all arms.

On the 23rd August, 1898, the *sirdar* held a general review of this imposing force at Wad Hamed, and company after company filed past the commander-in-chief, stirring the dust of the desert in dense clouds. Early on the 24th, the march south began. Rumours were rife in camp as to the *khalifa's* intentions and probable plan of action. It was thought by some that he would advance to meet our force in the open, by others that he would entrench himself in the fastness of Omdurman. His army was reported 45,000 strong.

Hajir was the first object of attainment by the British Army, a distance of 40 miles from Omdurman, and thence the route lay by Ker-

BATTLE OF OMDURMAN

reri, where a low range of sandstone hills inland led to the *khalifa's* city. The work of shifting quarters from point to point was characterised with the mechanical and infallible precision which marked every move of the *sirdar's* vast army. Writing from Wad Hamed about noon of the 26th August, the historian of the war says, "The camp is a wilderness of broken biscuit-boxes and battered jam tins"—where but a few hours before had been concentrated a force of 20,000 men.

Slowly the army marched south, and for a week its progress was uneventful. Moving in the form of a vast square, with sides a mile long, it crept nearer and ever nearer to Omdurman.

By the 28th, Gebel Royan, or Hajir, was reached, and from the hill overlooking the camp the Nile could be viewed almost up to Omdurman itself, and at this period the first *dervish* cavalry patrols were sighted. These, however, fell back without showing fight. The same day the gunboat *Zafir*, the flagship of Captain Keppel, sprang a leak and sank within a few moments. The utmost coolness was displayed by all on board, Captain Keppel being the last to leave, and no lives were lost, but the *Zafir* was, of course, rendered useless, and the naval commander's flag was transferred to the *Sultan*.

A striking example of the altered conditions of warfare in modern times is to be found in an observation of Mr. Steevens at this point:—

The correspondents would find the chief disadvantage of rain (of which the army had had by this time considerable experience) in the possible interruption of the field telegraph, which has been brought here, and will probably advance further.

An admirably-equipped field telegraph formed a not unimportant adjunct to the army's equipment. From now on, reconnaissances were of frequent occurrence, and on the 30th, some five Arab horsemen were overtaken and captured by Major Stuart-Wortley's friendlies, and shortly after wards the army reached Kerreri.

From this point Omdurman was clearly visible, "the *Mahdi's* tomb forming the centre of a purple stain on the yellow sand, going out for miles and miles on every side, a city worth conquering." Clearly visible, too, was the enemy's army, a long white line stretching in front of the city wall with a front of three miles.

On September 1st an admirable and final reconnaissance was effected, and the enemy's exact position and strength located. On the night of September 1st, the British Army bivouacked under arms at the village of Agaiga, fully expecting the *dervish* attack, but not until the morning of the 2nd did our scouts report the entire *dervish* army to be advancing against the British position. Their front was estimated at between three and four miles. Countless banners fluttered over their serried masses, and they chanted war-songs as they came steadily on.

Short and sharp came the orders from headquarters, and in a very short time the British Army had taken up its appointed position in front of its camp at Agaiga. On the left were the 2nd battalion Rifle Brigade, the Lancashire Fusiliers, the Northumberland Fusiliers, and the 1st battalion. Grenadier Guards, with the maxim battery manned by the Irish, Fusiliers. Then came the 1st battalion Royal Warwickshire regiment, the Cameron and Seaforth Highlanders, and the 1st battalion Lincolns in the order named, with a battery of maxims directed by the Royal Artillery.

The Soudanese brigades, under Generals Maxwell and Macdonald continued the fighting line, with the Egyptian brigades, under Generals Lewis and Collinson, in reserve. Captain Long had his maxim Nordenfelt batteries on both flanks. The British fighting line formed a large obtuse angle, with its convex side towards the enemy. Facing either flank of it were, on the British right, the heights of Kerreri, on their left the hill of Gebel Surgham. Between these two the enemy was now seen to be advancing.

About 6.30 a.m. the British opened fire with a suddenness which must have startled the advancing foe. Frightful was the execution done during these first, few moments of Omdurman. The foe were mown down in handfuls, yet fresh men ever rushed forward to fill their places, and still for a time they pressed forward.

Steevens says:—

No white troops could have faced that torrent of death for five minutes, but the Baggara and the blacks came on. The torrent of lead swept into them, and hurled them down in whole companies. You saw a rigid line gather itself up and rush on evenly; then, before a shrapnel shell or maxim the line suddenly quivered and stopped. The line was yet unbroken, but it was quite still. Sometimes they came near enough to see single figures quite plainly. One old man with a white nag started with five comrades; all dropped, but he alone came bounding forward to within 200 yards of the 14th Soudanese Then he folded his arms across his face, and his limbs loosened, and he dropped sprawling to earth beside his flag.

In such manner did the *Mahdists* fight their last great fight, but the issue of this, the first stage of the battle, was not long held in the balance. By eight o'clock firing ceased, the *dervishes* being by this time all out of range, and leaving scores of dead upon the field.

Half an hour later the advance was sounded, and in the order known as "echelon of brigades" the troops moved off towards Omdurman. As they approached the hill of Gebel Surgham a heavy *dervish* fire broke out, and it was then apparent that the *khalifa* had divided his army into three. The first portion had attacked the British camp at Agaiga in; front; the second, under Ali Wad Helu and the Sheik el Din, had moved towards Kerreri to envelop the British right; the third, under the *khalifa* himself, lay in wait behind Gebel Surgham, where they had bivouacked the previous night.

Both flanks were soon hotly engaged, and former scenes repeated. When the *dervishes* drew off behind the ridge in front of their camp, the *sirdar* detailed General Lewis's and General Collinson's Egyptian brigades, which up to this point had been held in reserve, to watch the attempt which the *dervishes* made to overwhelm our left, and meanwhile the cavalry were sent on in advance.

Just as the brigades reached the crest adjoining the Nile, the right, comprising the Egyptian brigades, marched out of camp and became engaged with the enemy. The action was now general. It was found that the *dervishes* had re-formed under cover of the rooky eminence two miles from camp, and had marched under the black standard of the *khalifa* in order to make a supreme effort to retrieve the fortunes of the day. Meanwhile a mass of about 15,000 strong bore down upon the two Egyptian brigades on our right. These, supported by a battery of maxims, succeeded in forming up steadily in order to face the *dervish* attack. The *sirdar* swung round his centre and left, leaving the 1st British Brigade with General Wauchope with the transport. General Maxwell's Soudanese brigade seized the rocky eminence, and General Macdonald's brigade joined the firing line.

In ten minutes—before the attack could be driven home—the flower of the *khalifa's* army was caught in a depression, and came under the withering crossfire of three brigades and their attendant artillery. Manfully the devoted *Mahdista* strove to make headway, but their rushes were swept away, and their main body mown through and through by the sustained and deadly fire of the *sirdar's* troops. Defiantly the *dervishes* planted their standards and died by them. It was more than human nature could bear, and after the dense mass had melted

172

to companies, and companies to driblets, they broke and fled, leaving the field white with *jibbah*-clad corpses, like a meadow dotted with snowdrifts.

Meanwhile on the left was taking place the great incident of the Battle of Omdurman—the fine charge of the 21st Lancers against enormous odds. Colonel Martin's orders were to prevent the broken enemy from returning to Omdurman, five miles away from the field of battle. The 21st Lancers unexpectedly came upon the enemy's reserves behind Gebel Surgham, who were 2,000 strong, but whose precise strength could not be ascertained owing to the nature of the ground. The cavalry were then in column of troops. They deployed into line for the attack, and charged. When they were within thirty yards of the enemy they found the latter, who had been ensconced in a *nullah*, and had been concealed by a depression of the ground.

Wild with excitement, coming on to the attack, the Lancers had not a single moment for hesitation. They charged gallantly home, the brunt of the business falling on No. 2 Squadron, who absolutely had to hack their way through the enemy, twenty deep, exposed as they were to a withering infantry fire. They struggled through, but every man who fell was immediately hacked to pieces by the swords of the fanatic foe. The men of the British cavalry rallied, bleeding and blown, on the far side of the lanes which they had cut for themselves in the enemy's ranks, and with admirable fortitude they re-formed as coolly as if they had been on parade.

One corporal who was covered with blood and reeling in his saddle, was yelling, "Fall in! fall in!" to the remnant of his company. "Fall out, corporal; you're wounded!" roared an officer. "No, sir! Fall in!" bawled the wounded man, waving his bent lance; "Form up, No. 2!" and No. 2 Squadron re-formed—four whole men all told.

Then it was that Lieutenant Grenfell was missed for the first time. Lieutenant de Montmorency, with Corporal Swarback, dashed out to effect, if possible, the rescue of his body. They were immediately joined by Captain Kenna. With their revolver fire the two officers kept the enemy forty yards away, and would have secured Lieutenant Grenfell's body if the horse upon which it was placed had not shied with its burden.

Seeing that a second charge would be futile, Colonel Martin dismounted his men, and with magazine and carbine fire drove the enemy steadily back into the zone of the Anglo-Egyptian infantry fire, the lancers having accomplished their object by covering the enemy's line of retirement, though at the cost of heavy casualties.

An eyewitness says:—

This maiden charge of the 21st Lancers, is regarded as an extremely brilliant affair.

All over the field the enemy were falling back before the tremendous fire of the British, but a last splendid stand was made by the *khalifa's* most devoted followers to the southwest of Gebel Surgham. Upon Macdonald fell the brunt of this last and most determined engagement. Suddenly the enemy poured down from Kerreri upon Macdonald's right, and for a moment, things looked critical.

To meet the attack, he turned his front through a complete half circle. Every tactician in the army was delirious in his praise. 'Cool as on parade' Macdonald was very much cooler. Beneath the strong square-hewn face you could tell that the brain was working as if packed in ice. He saw everything. Knew what to do. Did it. All saw him and knew they were being nursed to triumph."

The issue was not long; the British fire tremendous. Soon the enemy remaining fled in all directions, and the fight was won.

At a quarter past eleven the *sirdar* sounded the advance, and the whole force in line drove the scattered remnants of the foe into the desert, while the cavalry cut off their retreat to Omdurman. At 12.55 the Anglo-Egyptian column, preceded by the *sirdar* with the captured black standard of the *khalifa*, headed for Omdurman once more, this time unopposed.

The slaughter of Omdurman had been appalling. The *dervish* casualties reached the astonishing total of 11,000 killed, 16,000 wounded, and over 4,000 prisoners. The Anglo-Egyptian losses were phenomenally small, some 66 killed of all ranks in both forces—387 killed and wounded together. Such was the extraordinary disparity in the numbers. The *khalifa* himself escaped with the Sheik el Din to Omdurman. Ali Wad Helu was wounded. *Mahdism* was completely overthrown. The only *dervish* force now left in the field was that of the garrison of Gedaref up the Blue Nile. Here, some days later, Parsons Pasha, the Governor of Kassala, killed 700 of this number, and dispersed the rest, with a loss of only 37 killed.

No words can be too high in praise of the courage and discipline of the Egyptian troops. Led by such able men as Macdonald and Lewis, they had proved themselves first-class fighting men, and hearty congratulations were conveyed to all ranks from Her Majesty the Queen when the news of Omdurman became known in Britain.

Newspaper correspondents suffered heavily on the day of Omdurman. The Hon. Hubert Howard, acting for the *Times*, was killed by a bullet, but not till the end of the day. Colonel Rhodes, of the *Times*, and Mr. Williams, of the *Daily Chronicle*, were wounded. Mr. Cross, of the *Manchester Guardian*, died shortly afterwards of enteric fever—a heavy list in all.

Meanwhile the advance to Omdurman continued, and about two o'clock in the afternoon the city of the *khalifa* was reached. Here for some days past the gunboats had been doing considerable execution. The forts on Tuti Island had been totally demolished, and the dome of the *Mahdi's* tomb and the mosque of Omdurman partially destroyed. The destruction thus wrought became clearly visible as the British troops approached the city. They were met on the outskirts by "an old man on a donkey, with a white flag," and after some parley with the *sirdar*, and an assurance that the British would not put all the inhabitants to the sword, the way was continued into the heart of the city. Strange scenes were witnessed. Assured at length that the victors would not massacre and pillage, the inhabitants streamed out in their thousands, and, with shrill shouts of welcome, escorted the British soldiers through the streets.

Steevens says:—

Yet more wonderful were the women. The multitude of women whom concupiscence had harried from every recess of Africa and mewed up in Baggara *harems*, came out to salute their new masters. There were at least three of them to every man. Black women from Equatoria, and almost white women from Egypt. Plum-skinned Arabs, and a strange yellow type . . . the whole city was a monstrosity of African lust.

The capture of the *khalifa* himself was the one thought uppermost in every mind as the British troops streamed into Omdurman, and the *khalifa's* citadel was the first object of the quest. Here were found the numerous members of his bodyguard, but the leader himself had disappeared, slipping out of his conquered city, even as the white troops had marched in! All ranks were much chagrined by this failure to capture the wily dervish leader, but it was felt that his power was broken once and for all, as indeed proved to be the case.

175

The work of disarming his bodyguard proceeded apace, and very soon, finding they had little to fear from the victorious troops, the inhabitants of Omdurman set to work to loot the *khalifa's* corn. Among the captives released were Sister Teresa, a captive nun, who had been, forcibly married by the *khalifa's* orders to a Greek, and Charles Neufeld, a captive German merchant, who had suffered many years of imprisonment and brutality, and whose record of life in the *khalifa's* capital is full of interesting details and unique experiences.

By this time evening had set in, and all ranks were exhausted with the labours of the day, though the army continued to pour into Omdurman. The historian of the campaign says "Where the bulk of the army bivouacked, I know not, neither did they. I stumbled on the second British brigade, and there, by a solitary candle, the *sirdar*, flat on his back, was dictating his despatch to Colonel Wingate, flat on his belly. I scraped a short hieroglyphic scrawl on a telegraph form and fell asleep on the gravel with a half-eaten biscuit in my mouth."

On the 3rd September the majority of the army moved out to Khor Shamba, where they camped. The stench of Omdurman was found to be intolerable. Dead donkeys lay about the streets, and filth and squalor were perceptible om every side; the boasted capital of *Mahdism* proved to be little more than a vast collection of miserable hovels, and one and all were glad to be out of it, if only into the fresh air of the desert. Preparations were now made for one of the crowning acts of the campaign—the visible avenging of Gordon, who had died so nobly at Khartoum, distant less than two miles up the Nile.

Here, on the morning of Sunday, 4th September, the Union Jack and the Egyptian crescent were flung to the desert breeze, above the ruins of the Residency of Khartoum, half a dozen paces from the spot where Gordon died.

The *sirdar*, accompanied by the divisional generals, the brigadiers, and the full staffs, together with detachments from all branches of the Anglo-Egyptian Army, steamed up the Blue Nile to the ruins of Khartoum, early in the morning, and landed at the Masouri stage on the river bank opposite the Residency. Gordon's old palace, though gutted, was still intact in its foundations. On the summit of the dismantled walls two flagstaffs were raised, and detachments of representative troops, with the band of the 11th Soudanese regiment, the drums and fifes of the Grenadier Guards, and the pipes of the Highland regiments, formed up reverently round the historic spot, the gunboat *Melik* being made fast to the quay beside the Residency.

In the centre were the *sirdar* and his full personal staff, on the right the divisional generals and their staffs, and on the left a detachment of officers and sappers of the Royal Engineers—Gordon's old corps. The background was composed of the picturesque ruins of Khartoum, amid which were growing wild palms, acacias, and lemon trees.

At ten o'clock the *sirdar* gave the signal, and amid the crash of the first saluting gun and the opening strains of the British National Anthem, the personal *aide-de-camp* to the *sirdar* and Lieutenant Staveley unfurled the Union Jack. The Egyptian *aide-de-camp* to the *sirdar* and Major Nutford next hoisted the *Khedivial* Crescent, and thus the cry for vengeance heard for fifteen long years was for ever stilled. Amid the booming of the salutes and the rolling bars of the British and Khedivial National Anthems could be hoard the shrill cries of crowds of natives and slaves exulting at their emancipation, from cruel serfdom. Then the music changed. The Highland pipers wailed out a dirge, and the fifes of the Grenadier Guards played a dead march in memory of Gordon and of the heroes fallen in the late battle.

Now the chaplains to the forces—the Rev. J. M. Simms (Presbyterian), the Rev. A. W. B. Watson (Anglican), and the Rev. Robert Bundle (Roman Catholic), read appropriate passages of Scripture and prayers. The religious service was followed by the firing of 15 minute guns. The impressive and touching service was brought to a close; by the *sirdar* calling on the troops to give three cheers for Her Majesty the Queen-Empress and the *khedive*. They were given with a fervour which awoke the echoes for miles around.

What may be described as a side-ceremony then began. Fifes played the Dead March, pipes wailed a lament, and the band played Gordon's hymn, "Abide with me." When the solemn, music ceased all the general officers stepped forward and congratulated the *sirdar*, and half an hour was subsequently spent in visiting the chief historical points of the ruined city and the totally dilapidated remains of the steps on which Gordon was killed.

The *sirdar* then re-embarked and returned to camp. There were those who said that during the closing ceremonies he could hardly speak or see for emotion.

What wonder? He had trodden this road to Khartoum for fourteen years, and he stood at the goal at last. Thus, with Maxim, Nordenfelt, and Bible we buried Gordon after the manner of his race.

Of the subsequent advance through the former country of the *khalifa* a correspondent gives a vivid picture:—

If ever there were any who entertained a thought of pity for the *khalifa* and his following when they considered the crushing force which its advancing to their annihilation, if they could have been with us upon the road during the last few days, all thought of sentiment and pity would have vanished, and even the most philanthropical would have longed, as do we, to volunteer our aid in ridding the world of a tyrant so brutal and a butcher so ferocious.

All along the line of march there are evidences that the country was once a flourishing, populous province, well cultivated where occasion offered. Yet to us it was a wilderness of desolation, every mile with its evidences of the tragic means by which it had been depopulated, and every landmark showing the handiwork of the ruthless destroyer. From end to end it has been swept with fire and sword. The very crops have grown, withered, and died without a hand to gather them.

Mile after mile of earthen village lies deserted, ruined and destroyed, and now in the courtyards where the women were wont to grind corn and card cotton, with their children playing at their skirts, jackal and hyena disport amongst the broken distaffs and the bones of the murdered women and butchered infants. Well may we cry, 'Retribution and Khartoum!'

CHAPTER 18

The Advance of Roberts: 1900

The war of 1899-1901 in South Africa is of too recent date to call for a very minute exposition of the causes which led up to it.

The first appearance of the Dutch in South Africa took place in 1652. On the invitation of the Netherlands Government, Britain seized Cape Colony in 1795, holding it for a period of seven years, when it was restored to the Netherlands. Five years later Britain again seized it, and it was finally ceded to them upon a payment of £6,000,000. From this time forward strife commenced between the Boers and the British immigrants. English was the language chosen for the law courts of Cape Colony, and all slaves of whom the Boers held many thousands, were freed under British rule. Both these happenings gave great offence, and in 1836 the Boers made their "Great Trek" into new territory.

Says Mr. Julian Ralph in his history of the late war:—

Great Britain never ceased to regard the Boers as her subjects, and yet did nothing to interfere with their course or the government which they set up.

In 1852, after many bickerings, the famous Sand River Convention established the Transvaal Republic, over which Great Britain "held the right to impose conditions, upon which she granted the Boers what rights they held, and this British overlordship was acknowledged by them without protest." The Orange Free State was set up under somewhat similar conditions, with, however, somewhat more extended privileges than those enjoyed by the Transvaal. The Transvaal Government went from bad to worse.

Frequent friction with the natives. marked by savage cruelties on both sides, and the virtual enslaving of many natives, brought the Government of the Transvaal into disrepute, and in 1877 the British Commissioner, Sir Theophilus Shepstone, formally annexed the Transvaal, reporting that the majority of people desired annexation. Protests were, however, numerous, and shortly after order had been apparently restored the newly-annexed territory revolted, defeating the British forces at Laing's Nek and Majuba Hill, in what has become known to posterity as the First Boer War.

An armistice was ordered by Mr. Gladstone's Government in March, 1881, and the Boers were granted self-government under British suzerainty. Further independence was granted to them in 1884.

The discovery of gold in the Transvaal Republic had by this time led to a great rush of new settlers, called by the Boers, the "*Uitlanders*," to whose energy the present prosperity of the country was now largely due. These European settlers, the *Uitlanders*, were of course subject to the laws of the Transvaal, and very soon they found that instead of possessing equal rights with Transvaal *burghers*, though forming nearly three-fourths of the white population, they were at disadvantages in everyway. Dutch was the only language of government, and was taught in the public schools. British citizens were assaulted, and even murdered by agents of the Transvaal with impunity, and right of franchise was refused.

The *Uitlanders* determined on revolt, and a somewhat premature movement was made by Dr. Jameson, in his famous, and of course disastrous, raid. Negotiations now ensued, and Sir Alfred Milner, the High Commissioner at the Cape, held many meetings with President Kruger of the Transvaal, with a view to securing fair and equal rights for the *Uitlanders*. The sequel is fresh in the minds of all. Prevarications, endless delays, and abortive conferences followed the Boers all the while arming themselves for the forthcoming conflict which they had virtually decided upon. The British yoke was to be thrown off once and for all.

Gradually Britain massed her forces in South Africa, and when finally, on the 9th October, 1899, the Boer Government presented a virtual ultimatum, war became inevitable. The ultimatum protested against the right of the British Government to interfere in the affairs of the Transvaal. It demanded the withdrawal from South Africa of the British reinforcements, and it desired an answer to these demands before 5 p.m. on the day in question. The British reply was brief and to the point; it merely announced that Her Majesty's Government had no further announcement to make to Mr. Kruger.

At first the British preparations were wholly inadequate. Some

20,000 British troops in all were available on the spot, but a complete army corps of 50,000 men, under Sir Redvers Buller, was mobilised in Britain and despatched at once. Divisional commanders were Lord Methuen, Sir William Gatacre, and Sir Francis Clery. The opening engagement of the war took place on October 12th, when an armoured train, conveying cannon to Mafeking was attacked, and several men were captured. On November 1st, the Free State Boers, siding with their Transvaal brethren, invaded Cape Colony.

To relieve Kimberley, Ladysmith, and Mafeking, where the frontier garrisons were enclosed on all sides by the enemy, now became the objective of the campaign. Lord Methuen moved from the Orange River for the relief of Kimberley, and on November 23rd, with the Guards and the 9th Brigade, drove 2,500 Boers out of their entrenched position at Belmont with the bayonet. Two days later, at Enslin, near Graspan, a memorable battle was fought against 3,000 Boers, and the British, though successful, lost heavily—14 killed and 91 wounded out of a total force of 550 men.

On November 28th the Battle of Modder River, against 8,000 Boers, was fought. Ten hours' fighting under a burning sun resulted in the British holding their own, but with a loss of 4 officers and 71 men killed, and 19 officers and 375 men wounded. On the 11th December, Lord Methuen's force fought a fierce engagement at Magersfontein, to the north of Modder River, where General Cronje had prepared a long series of concealed entrenchments. The British force numbered 11,000, the Boers 15,000, strongly entrenched. The Highland Brigade, marching in quarter column in the dusk of early morning found itself close to the barbed wire obstructions of the strongest entrenchments, and a tremendous rifle fire at close range greeted the hardy Scotsmen.

Nothing could exceed their gallantry, but no troops could stand against that awful blast, and one man in every five of the 3,000 led by General Wauchope was mown down. The gallant Wauchope himself fell, riddled by bullets, at the head of his men, a brave and well-beloved soldier. For the whole day the fight raged, but it was found impossible to dislodge the Boers, and a retreat to Modder River was inevitable. The British losses were more than 850 casualties the killed alone totalled 152, and 130 men reported missing.

Meanwhile General Gatacre had begun operations in Cape Colony north of Queenstown. He occupied Bushmen's Hock on November 27, while his main force was at Buller's Kraal. On December 10th, the day before Magersfontein, he met with a sad reverse in making a night attack on Stormberg, when he was misled by guides and at daybreak was surprised by the enemy. Five hundred of his force were cut off and made prisoners. All attempts to reach Ladysmith had been fruitless.

General Symons, acting under Lieut.-General White at Ladysmith, occupied Dundee and Glencoe, and fought the first serious battle, of the Natal campaign on October 20th, in an attack on Lucas Myer's army, 6,000 strong, who held an advantageous position on Talana Hill. At the cost of his own life, General Symons accomplished a successful issue. The Boers were driven from their guns, and these were captured. The next day a fierce engagement was fought at Elandslaagte. General French's cavalry and the Gordon Highlanders played conspicuous parts, and a heavy defeat to the enemy resulted.

Four British officers and 37 men were killed; the wounded of all ranks totalled over 200. The Boer losses were put at 100 killed, 108 wounded, including General Kock, and nearly 200 prisoners. Generals White and Yule now joined forces in Ladysmith, which was at once invested by the enemy. Disaster now overtook the relieving force. At Nicholson's Nek nearly 900 officers and men were taken prisoners. On December 15th General Buller fought a fierce battle with the enemy at Colenso, and lost eleven guns, having 1,097 officers and men killed, wounded, and missing. Operations were now brought to a standstill.

Few will forget that dark December day when check after check to the British forces in South Africa announced the war was at a standstill, and little forward movement could be made until the hands of our commanders had been strengthened, and that, too, considerably. The disasters did much to bring out the national doggedness and determination. From every county and every colony, from remote Highland hamlets and from the teeming cities of the Empire the flower of Britain went forth to do battle for her honour in South Africa, and the government, at length convinced of the arduous nature of the enterprise, lent an able assistance to the national will and determination.

On December 23rd, 1899, Field-Marshal Lord Roberts of Kandahar left London for Cape Town, to take supreme command of the British Armies in South Africa, and he was joined at Gibraltar by his chief of staff, Lord Kitchener of Khartoum, who had travelled post haste from Egypt. A sigh of relief went up on every side when these two able and distinguished officers, backed by a vast and ever-increasing army, took up the reins of war in the disordered kingdoms.

Matters now began to mend slowly. A detachment of 120 colonial mounted infantry, on December 30th, under Captain Montmorency, were cut off near Dordrecht, and for a whole night held out gallantly against a force of 800 of the enemy. In the morning they were relieved by a party of the Cape Mounted Rifles. The next day General French conducted successful operations near Colesberg, and on the 1st of January he shelled their position, compelling them to fall back. The same day Colonel Pilcher defeated a commando at Sunny side.

With such small successes the arrival of Lord Roberts was heralded, and every day reinforcements poured into South Africa. A desperate attempt was made on the 6th January to overwhelm Ladysmith, but after 17 hours' fighting, the foe were driven back with heavy loss.

The turning point of the war, however, was reached when, on January 10th, 1900, Roberts took charge of hostilities, and began his famous march to Pretoria. A month after his arrival at Cape Town, Lord Roberts and his staff went north, his movements being shrouded in mystery. On the 9th February, 1900, he took over command at Modder River camp, and within three days his great movement was begun. The Highland Brigade, under the bravest of soldiers, Major-General Macdonald, were engaged with the enemy to the west of the railway, this being to attract the enemy's attention from the preparation for a greater event.

The intention was to make straight to relieve Kimberley. Suddenly the Free State (as it was then) was invaded at various points to the south of Modder River. General French, who had been withdrawn from Colesberg with his cavalry, dashed north, brushing aside or ignoring small parties of Boers, who sought to oppose him. The general then swept in a circle round the east of Magersfontein, and after a trying march, Kimberley was reached late in the afternoon of Wednesday, February 14th.

The Boer commandoes had timely warning of the advancing hosts, and, recognising that in the circumstances their position was untenable, the enemy took to flight. There was very little fighting. The Kimberley garrison moved out when it was apparent that the relief force was at hand, but the enemy did not wait for these. The garrison was too late to intercept the retreat, the Boers getting away in the darkness. The Boers' loss in arms and ammunition was enormous. The first of the besieged towns had been relieved, but not at a cheap price. It was work which cost Britain, from Belmont onwards, 129 officers and 1,818 men. The British infantry brigades followed in the wake

LORD ROBERTS ENTERING IN KIMBERLEY

of General French, and marching north-east, occupied Jacobsdal, the Boer base of supplies.

General Cronje, one of the most stubborn of the Boer generals, whose tactic were typical of his reputed border ancestry, saw that he ran a great risk of being surrounded in his trenches at Magersfontein. There was one loophole of escape—to the east between the rear of the British cavalry and the front of the infantry. Accordingly, Cronje warily made towards Bloemfontein by this route. But he was not circumspect enough, and his retreat was soon discovered. British infantry and cavalry were despatched in hot pursuit, and he was brought to bay on the 10th at Paardeberg, in the valley of the Modder River. On that day an attempt to storm the Boer *laager* failed.

The British circled round the doomed Cronje, and day by day the lines of investment were drawn closer. Shot and shell were poured into the camp of the Boers, who, like rabbits, buried themselves in holes in the river bank. Quite a number of Boer commandoes were defeated, but despite this, and the fact that his camp was in flames, and shot and shell were dropping into it like rain, the obstinate Cronje refused to yield. The statement that Cronje was a descendant of the old raiders of Galloway was certainly amply qualified by his tactics throughout. However, on the morning of Majuba Day—27th February—the Canadians, Gordons, and Shropshires dashed forward, and entrenched themselves in a position which commanded the Boer camp. After this, Cronje saw that further resistance was useless, and, with 4,000 men, unconditionally surrendered.

It was a small force that was commanded by Cronje as compared with the army of besiegers, and he had held out magnificently. After the battle an examination of the enemy's position showed this. The whole of the river on both sides was honeycombed with trenches, but such trenches as had never before been used in warfare; they were really underground dwellings, and perfectly secure unless a shell was dropped into the opening above. Straight projecting missiles were bound to fail to have an effect.

The condition of the whole *laager*, and trenches, however, was a frightful one. Every three paces lay dead horses, mules and cattle, polluting the air, and it was no wonder Cronje was forced to surrender at last. The parting between several men and their wives at this stage was extremely heartrending, and both were crying bitterly. The completeness of the capture was the more singular in view of the determined character of the enemy, and it was thought, at the very least, the enemy would destroy their guns and ammunition before surrendering.

The pursuit and capture of the Boers cost Britain no fewer than 98 officers and 1,436 men.

Pushing on from Paardeberg, Lord Roberts, on the 7th March, outflanked the Boers at Poplar Grove, compelling them to retreat, and three days later he defeated them at Driefontein. Ex-President Steyn fled from the capital, and on the 13th, Lord Roberts took possession, as he himself put it, "by the help of God and the bravery of Her Majesty's soldiers." The total casualties, since the army left Modder River, were 2,086 officers and men, killed, wounded and missing.

The occupation of Bloemfontein had a wonderful effect on the course of events. The Boers withdrew from northern Cape Colony, and the British forces crossed the Orange River on 15th March. There had been much desultory fighting in this district, and the British losses would amount to about 2,000.

While the relief of Ladysmith by General Buller was taking place, Lord Roberts rested at Bloemfontein for six weeks for the purpose of re-organising his transport service, and generally strengthening his forces. This inactivity on the part of the British commander was fully taken advantage of by the Boers, who swept down to the east and south-east of the capital. It was then Lord Roberts decided to check the enemy's progress, and the Battle of Karree was fought, at which the enemy made their last stand between Bloemfontein and Brandfort.

Their attitude had become unceasingly aggressive, and if the Free State *burghers*, who had surrendered to Britain, were to be assured of her ability to protect them, it was necessary to check the raids and incursions in the country immediately north of the capital. Lord Roberts deputed this task to the 7th Division, commanded by Lieutenant-General Tucker, the 1st and 3rd cavalry brigade under General French, and the brigade of mounted infantry under Colonel le Gallais.

At an early hour in the morning the whole force, preceded by a screen of mounted men, moved out of the advance camp in the direction of a ridge which commanded the line of railway north of Modder Bridge. It was known to be occupied and entrenched by an outpost of 1,500 Boers. Moving forward over the plain, which the British cavalry had already reconnoitred, General Tucker was soon in front of the enemy's position. After a stiff fight and attacks from various positions, the object of the advance was fully attained, and the troops bivouacked on the position they had carried. The Boers, however, succeeded in getting away over a flat country with all their guns and waggons.

This was followed by several rather unfortunate mishaps to the British forces at Sanna's Post and Reddersburg, the latter being particularly noted for a gallant stand by the Royal Irish Rifles against great odds. Three companies of Royal Irish Rifles and two companies of the north regiment of mounted infantry which had been captured by the Boers, were falling back for a position when they were surrounded by over 3,000 of the enemy, occupying a *kopje*. They defended the position for nearly 24 hours, notwithstanding that they were without food or water, and were exposed to the shells of the enemy's guns. This fight was one of rifles on the Boer side and artillery on the other, and before darkness fell all the gallant British fellows were being led away.

General Gatacre, who had been advised of the fighting, hurried to the scene, to arrive two hours late. At this time the whole country was reeking with active spies. As a result of Reddersburg about 600 men were captured. While at Sanna's Post, another unfortunate mishap, 37 officers and over 500 men were made prisoners. After this came the stiff engagement at Wepener, which lasted several days. An attempt was made to encircle the enemy by the British general, and while the opposing forces received a check, both sides suffered heavy casualties. This attempt at encircling the enemy was not successful.

The end of April found Lord Roberts' preparations finished, and the opening days of May witnessed the beginning of the triumphal march north. The British front extended across country for forty miles, and time and again overlapped the *burgher* flanks and threatened their lines of retreat. After several days' hard marching, during which splendid progress was made, Kronstad was reached, and here great opposition was expected. Great preparations had been made by Lord Roberts to make his march a successful one, and before the rapid advance of the British forces the Boers fled in confusion from the position at Kronstad. No fewer than 10,000 of them passed through the town the night previous to the arrival of the British forces, quite a number of the residents following. The enemy had been reinforced by 3,000 men from Natal, but the position they took up was quite untenable, and they beat a retreat.

Thus, no fewer than 128 miles had been covered by Lord Roberts' forces in about twelve days' time. For a week the forces rested at Kronstad, and getting ready for the march again, an advance was made towards the Transvaal. On the 23rd May the forces arrived at

Rhenoster River, where again they were surprised in finding the enemy had gone, having fled during the night of our arrival. The enemy had occupied a strong position on the north bank of the river, which had been carefully entrenched, but they did not think it advisable to defend it when they heard that General Hamilton's force was at Heilbron, and the cavalry, which crossed the Rhenoster, some miles lower down the stream, was threatening their right rear.

Right on from here the British march to the Vaal was made with great progress, and although the enemy threatened strong resistance on several occasions, they always retreated in front of the British forces, and evacuated their strongholds. On the queen's birthday, 24th May, the British forces entered the Transvaal, and encamped on the north bank. The advance troops, who crossed first, were only just in time to save the coal mines on each side of the river from being destroyed. The river was crossed amid loud cheer? by Compton's Horse and the Dorset Company, who were fired at by several scouting parties of Boers. These were pursued, and had a very narrow escape from being captured.

General Botha had considered the line of the Vaal indefensible, and the big guns were taken to Pretoria. After this it was becoming more and more evident that the Boer forces were shrinking at the thought of opposing such an army as General Roberts led, and on May 28th, when Klip River, which is 18 miles from Johannesburg, was reached, the enemy, who had prepared several positions, where they intended to set up opposition, again fled, or abandoned one after another: their vantage grounds. So hard were the enemy pressed on this occasion, that they had only time to get their guns into the train, and leave the station when some of the mounted infantry dashed into it

The complete success of Lord Roberts' march seemed now only a matter of time, but there was no falling off in the desire to press forward as quickly as possible the more so seeing the enemy wore being hustled out of their various positions. On the Tuesday following their arrival at Klip River, the British forces arrived at a point about ten miles from Johannesburg, without any serious opposition. The enemy were completely taken aback, as they did not expect the arrival until next day, and had not even carried off all the rolling stock. On the Thursday Johannesburg was in the hands of the British.

Lord Roberts, on the Wednesday, had summoned the town to surrender within twenty-four hours. The Boer *commandant* considered this course inadvisable, as the town was full of *burghers*, but these difficulties were overcome, and the field-marshal entered and hoisted the British flag. The entry of Lord Roberts into Johannesburg has been described as a spectacle to be remembered by all who beheld it. After formally accepting the surrender of the town, Lord Roberts left the building, and, remounting his charger, proceeded to the next ceremony, which, was the hauling down of the Transvaal flag. Numbers of the rugged *burghers* who were witnesses to this action appeared touched to the heart. When the flag was lowered tears were seen streaming down the faces of several men as they looked at the loss of all they had been fighting for during many weary months. While the National Anthem was being sung, a tall Free Stater, an artillerist, refused to remove his hat, and a fellow-spectator, a small man, attempted to pull it off, whereupon a British soldier standing near pushed the aggressor away, saying,

Leave him alone. He fought for his flag; you fight for none.

Lord Roberta took up his quarters at a small inn with the sign "Orange Grove," and here a rather interesting anecdote is recorded, the truth of which has, however, been denied by the principal actor.

Early in the evening, soon after the field-marshal reached his quarters, one of the officers of the staff approached him in order to discuss a matter of importance. He found the field-marshal with one of the innkeeper's little children on his knee, trying to teach the mite to trace the letters of the alphabet. When the officer entered, Lord Roberts looked up with a smile and said, "Don't come now; can't you see I'm busy!"

Only 30 miles now separated the British forces from Pretoria After the taking of Johannesburg, the people began to lose all confidence in their leaders, and during the short period that the troops stayed in the town, large numbers of the Boers came forward and surrendered. After hearing that Lord Roberts had reached Johannesburg, Kruger joined the retreat. Gathering up his goods and chattels, the ex-President, leaving his ignorant and deluded *burghers* to their fate, scuttled ignominiously out of the country.

Continuing his march forward, General Roberts made straight for Pretoria for his crowning effort. On the way a number of lingering parties of Boers were met, and these were driven off to surrounding hills. On Monday, the 4th June, the troops started on what was supposed to be their final march. After going about ten miles, however, the district of Six Mules Spruit was found to be occupied by the enemy. Two companies of the mounted infantry, along with four companies of the Yeomanry, were despatched to the scene, and quickly dislodged the enemy from the south bank.

After pursuing them for nearly a mile, the companies found themselves under a heavy fire from guns, which the Boers had placed on a well-concealed and commanding position. The British heavy guns, naval and Royal Artillery, which had been purposely placed in the front part of the column, were hurried on to the assistance of the mounted infantry as fast as oxen and mules could travel over the great rolling hills by which Pretoria is surrounded. The guns were supported by Stephenson's Brigade, and after firing a few rounds they drove the enemy out of their positions

The Boers then attempted to turn the British left flank. In this they were again foiled by the mounted infantry, and Yeomanry, supported by Maxwell's Brigade and Tuckers Division. As they still kept pressing on the left rear, General Roberts sent word for Ian Hamilton, who was advancing three miles to the left, to incline his forces and fill up the gap between the two columns. This finally checked the enemy, who were driven back towards Pretoria. General Roberta was expecting that he might have been able to follow them, and as the days were then very short in that part, and after nearly twelve hours' marching and fixating, the troops had to bivouac on the ground fought over during the day.

Just before dark the enemy were beaten back from nearly all the positions they had been holding, and Ian Hamilton's mounted infantry followed them up within 2,000 yards of Pretoria, through which they retreated hastily. Colonel de Lisle then sent an officer with a flag of truce into the town, demanding its surrender.

Shortly before midnight Lord Roberts was awakened by two officials of the South African Republic—Sandburg, military secretary to General Botha, and a general officer of the Boer army—who brought him a letter from Commandant Botha, proposing an armistice for the purpose of settling terms of surrender. Lord Roberts replied that he would gladly meet the commander-general the next morning, but that he was not prepared to discuss any terms, as the surrender of the town must be unconditional. At the same time his lordship asked for a reply by daybreak, as he had ordered the troops to march on the town as soon as it was light.

In his reply, Botha stated that he had decided not to defend Pretoria, and that he trusted the women, children and property would be protected. About one o'clock in the morning Lord Roberts was met by three principal civil officials with a flag of truce, stating their wish to surrender the town. At two o'clock in the afternoon of the 5th June, 1900, Pretoria was occupied by His Majesty's troops, and nearly 4,000 British prisoners of war were released.

But the occupation of Pretoria was not to see the termination of the war. May 17th had seen Mafeking relieved by Colonels Mahon and Plumer, and cordial was the welcome extended to these officers by its harassed garrison and by its brave defender Colonel Baden-Powell. For six months and six days the gallant defenders had held out. On February 26th Ladysmith had been relieved, after a siege of nearly four months. General Buller making a formal entry on the 2nd March; but much yet remained to be done elsewhere, and a species of guerilla warfare ensued.

On July 31st, Generals Hunter and Rundle captured the Boer leader Prinsloo with 4,000 of his men, but De Wet, the wily and mobile head of the Boer cavalry forces, still remained at large, and for nearly 18 months the war dragged on its weary course, the block-house system of Lord Kitchener, now in supreme command, gradually reducing the number of the foe in the field.

Peace was finally signed at Pretoria on May 31st, 1902, both the Transvaal and Orange Free State having been formally annexed by the British Empire.

No less than 1,072 officers and 20,870 non-commissioned officers and men had died in the field, either from wounds or disease, whilst the total Boer losses will probably never be known.

CHAPTER 19

The Battle of Jidballi: 1904

To say that the story of Somaliland lies before it, is, at first sight, to make a self-evident and apparently obvious assertion. But undoubtedly the future of the country will constitute by far the most important part of its history. The "Unknown Horn of Africa" was but recently, and is indeed still, a barbarous land whose tale is yet to be told. Day by day, however, the story is being added to, and this out-of-the-way district of Africa is at the present receiving an amount of attention from European Powers which will ensure it, ere long, an important and prosperous development.

As early as 1840 treaties with the native chiefs of this tract of land opposite Aden had been concluded by the British. Between 1873-77 the country was practically annexed by Egypt, but was given up and eventually occupied by the British in 1885, who declared a Protectorate over it, to the great satisfaction of its inhabitants. The reasons for such occupation were obvious—partly to save the country from relapsing into barbarism, and partly to prevent its occupation by other Powers, by which the overland route to the east might be menaced. Such Powers were France, Italy, and Abyssinia. The outcome of conferences between these Powers—with France in 1888, Italy in '91 and '94, and Abyssinia in '97—fixed the boundaries of the Somali Coast Protectorate.

So far, the story of Somaliland development was a peaceful one, and the commerce of the country in skins and hides, ostrich feathers, gums, cattle and sheep bade fair to grow and flourish to the profit of all concerned.

In 1899, however, the name of the *Mullah* began to be first heard. In that year Haji Mohammed Abdullah, a strict Moslem and Somali patriot, started a fanatical movement in the Dolbahanta country against both British and Abyssinian rule.

For several months, however, apathy marked the attitude of the British Government towards the *Mullah* and his following. It was thought that the rebellion would in all probability come to nothing, and nothing was accordingly done to check it. The issue proved the contrary, and as the *Mullah's* following increased and he now and again moved within a threatening distance of Berbera, the principal port, it was felt that something must be done. The Abyssinians were the first to make a move, and, massing a large army, they fought a sanguinary battle in the Ogaden country against the forces of the *Mullah* at Jig-gigga. The immediate outcome of this engagement was to drive the *Mullah* towards Berbara, and once more his presence in the vicinity, and his frequent daring raids, had the effect of unsettling the countryside.

Accordingly, in 1901, Colonel Swayne, the Consul General of the Protectorate, took the field with a small force, but with most unfortunate results. It has been suggested that not only was the force at Colonel Swayne's disposal totally inadequate, but that his appeals to the Foreign Office did not receive the backing they merited; in any event, disaster overtook the small expeditionary force. Not at first, however. On June 1st the column reached Sanala, and captured much of the enemy's livestock. Leaving a *zareba* under Captain Macneil with 300 men, Colonel Swayne moved against the *Mullah's* camp at Yahol. The. *zareba* meantime was fiercely attacked, but gallantly defended, and the enemy driven off. Further operations resulted in the breakup of the *Mullah's* force, but the *Mullah* himself escaped across the Baud desert, where pursuit was, under the circumstances, impossible.

A period of comparative quiet followed, extending to nearly six months, but at length, in December, 1901, the *Mullah* once more resumed his operations against the friendly tribes. Colonel Swayne again got together a force, but while operating between Bohotte and Mudug sustained a severe reverse at Erego. Two officers, Colonel Phillips and Captain Angus, with 50 men, were killed, and the British wounded numbered over 100. The force was attacked in the thick bush, and the Somali levies were severely shaken by the savage onslaught of the *Mullah's* men. Under the circumstances Colonels Swayne and Cobbe, the latter wounded in the engagement, decided to retreat to Bohotte.

Not a little anxiety was occasioned at home over this setback, and the immediate outcome of Colonel Swayne's urgent entreaty for more men was the despatch of large reinforcements under General Manning. Such measures were felt to be especially necessary, as a Hungarian adventurer ("of the worst type," says one account) was reported to be directing the *Mullah's* forces, and would assuredly make the most of the British reverse. This report was, however, discredited. In any event, large reinforcements were now despatched to Berbera; Bombay Grenadiers from Aden, and Bombay Infantry from Simla, Soudanese and Sikhs, with maxims and many extra officers—all were hastened to the scene of war.

General Manning himself set foot in Berbera on the morning of the 22nd October, and at once all was renewed activity. The campaign, however, was destined to be a failure, owing to inefficient transport, the service of which utterly broke down, and also to the great daring and activity of the opposing force, whose fighting qualities had been seriously underestimated.

As far on as April 15th, 1903, advices reached this country from Somaliland, telling of successful reconnaissances and bright prospects of success, but two days later, on the 17th, and again on the 23rd of the month, two such severe blows were inflicted on the large British force now in the field as to render a second withdrawal from the country necessary. Colonel Plunkett, in charge of a strong party of the King's African Rifles with maxims, set out from Galadi in the direction of Walwal, on the 15th of the month for the purpose of rounding-up stock in the bush.

After marching 40 miles, the force left its spare kit and maxims, and pushed on after the carriers, who, with the cattle, were following the *Mullah's* rear. On the 17th the force was surrounded by the enemy and cut to pieces. No fewer than 10 officers and 174 men were killed, among them Colonel Plunkett himself. The enemy's force was estimated at 80,000, of whom they left 2,000 dead on the field. Only 41 of the little British force managed to reach camp, six alone being unwounded. Both maxims fell into the *Mullah's* hands. A force under Colonel Cobbe in the vicinity was, with the greatest difficulty, extricated by General Manning, who left Bohotte at midnight on hearing of the disaster.

But alas! this was not all. A week later, on the 23rd, the flying column under Major Gough, operating to the north, was attacked with a loss of two officers, Captains Godfrey and Bruce, and 13 men. With the greatest difficulty it reached Bohotte, and here the 1902 campaign came to a disastrous termination.

Small wonder that considerable dissatisfaction should by this time have arisen at home over the conduct of the Somaliland campaign. The question of withdrawal from the country was even mooted, but

BATTLE OF JIDBALLI

fortunately overruled, and a still stronger force was once more got together to initiate the campaign which is at the present time (1904) in progress.

Meanwhile the *Mullah* sustained a trifling defeat at the hands of an Abyssinian force on the 31st May, the remains of the British expedition being still at Bohotte, where they were detained until plans of reinforcement and advance had been duly organised.

On the 21st June Major-General Sir C. Egerton was appointed to command the Somaliland expeditionary force.

Shortly after the general's arrival at Berbera, active and most strenuous preparations were made for an expedition which should at last succeed in overthrowing the *Mullah's* power. Several months were spent in these preparations. Reinforcements began to arrive in large quantities at Berbera; from Simla came Mounted Infantry and Punjaubees, companies of the Norfolk and Yorkshire regiments, Mounted Infantry from Bombay, 300 of the Hampshire regiment from Aden, a telegraph battalion of the Royal Engineers from Lorne, two companies of the Army Service Corps from Durban, Natal, and even a strong contingent from the newly-formed Boer colony in South Africa, with camels and transport materials, and all the munitions of war poured into Somaliland in a steady stream.

Sheikh was chosen as a first base of concentration, and later this was advanced to Kurit, where there is a capital and abundant water supply. Lack of water indeed has constituted one of the chief difficulties attending operations in Somaliland—the possessor of the somewhat infrequent wells being master of the situation. Transport, too, is of even greater importance than ever in such a country, Somali camels alone being found thoroughly suitable for the purpose. Many thousands of other camels were imported into the country, but it was found that they stood the climate ill, and in many instances were totally useless.

Under the circumstances, the local supply had to be mainly depended upon, and as this proved to be wholly inadequate, the best had to be done under adverse circumstances. In due course, however, garrisons were established at Bohotte, Ganero, and Burao, and early in December the general issued a proclamation to the tribes that operations were about to commence, and abjured them to preserve a loyal and helpful attitude to the British arms.

On the 19th December occurred the first fight of any importance. On that date Colonel Kenna, moving out of Eil Dab, on a reconnaissance, came on 2,000 of the enemy at Jidballi at the head of the

Nogal Valley. Fierce fighting ensued, the enemy losing 80 killed and nearly 100 wounded. The British loss was two of the Tribal horse killed. These troops fought with conspicuous gallantry, and earned the special commendation of their British leaders. After the engagement, Colonel Kenna fell back upon the main body as the *Mullah* was reported to be in force in the Nogal Valley.

Such indeed proved to be the case. On January 11th was fought what may be described as an important battle at Jidballi, the enemy losing over 1,000 killed, and retreating considerably shaken. At nine o'clock on the morning of the 11th, General Egerton advanced upon the enemy's position. Leaving the heavy transport in a *zareba*, 12 miles in the rear, the force advanced in the following order.

The 1st and 2nd Brigades, commanded respectively by Generals Manning and Fasken, marched in one large square, covered by a screen of Illaloe natives on the front. The advance guard was composed of the Gadabursi horse, with the Somali mounted infantry. On the south flank was Major Kenna with two companies of British and three companies of Indian mounted infantry. The Tribal horse, supported by the Bikauirs, had been sent from the north flank to work round the enemy's rear to prevent them making a way to the east or north.

Slowly the British force worked up towards the enemy's position— a deep *nullah* directly in front of the line of march. Nearer and nearer came the attacking party, until within 700 yards of the position. Suddenly the *Mullah's dervishes* swept down with wild cries, and hurled themselves towards the square. They never reached it. From rifle and maxim swept forth such a fire as must have astounded those who lived to recall it. For ten minutes an awful hurricane of bullets hurled back the *Mullah's* soldiers, and then, doubly bewildered by the flank attack of the mounted troops, they turned and fled. The attempt to rush the square had failed. It was the only one they made. Losing heart under the terrific storm of lead, they scattered, helpless and disordered, in all directions. Three hundred lay dead upon the field.

Major Kenna's mounted infantry now took a hand in the engagement, and for two hours inflicted severe punishment on the fugitives at short range, killing over 500, as they fled hither and thither, and only pausing when his horses were worn out for lack of water, and ammunition began to run short.

The *Mullah's* army at Jidballi was estimated at 5,000 men, of whom they left, as stated, 1,000 dead behind their line of flight. The *Mullah* himself, who was a few miles distant, escaped. But the victory had cost us dear. Three officers, including Lieutenants C. H. Bowden-Smith and V. R. Welland, were killed, together with nine of the native troops, whilst the wounded officers numbered nine, and other wounded 22. The total British force numbered 3,200 of all ranks.

Captain the Hon. T. Lister, of the 10th Hussars, who was at first reported missing, was found also to have been killed. He was the eldest son of Lord Ribbledale—a young man of five and twenty.

Thus ended the fight at Jidballi, a position which the *Mullah* had ordered his forces to hold to the last, and there can be no doubt that the effect of the victory was far-reaching, if indeed it did not succeed in shattering the morale of his troops. Meanwhile, the pursuit of the fugitive was actively proceeded with.

CHAPTER 20

The Battle at Hot Springs: 1904

For a series of years matters had been in an unsatisfactory state between Thibet and the Indian Government. This was caused by the non-fulfilment of treaty obligations on the part of the former. The Indian Government made long-continued efforts to bring matters to a proper understanding, but all without result. These efforts were frustrated by combined duplicity on the part of the Llamas of Thibet and of the Chinese authorities. The Thibet and Chinese authorities having repeatedly failed to fulfil their promise of sending properly-authorised deputies to settle matters of dispute and disagreement, the Indian Government at last felt compelled to send a political agent to the seat of Thibetan authority in order to have proper parties to deal with.

Accordingly, Colonel Younghusband was despatched for that purpose, but for his protection he required a military escort. The progress of the party was reported from time to time, everything going on peacefully, when the country was startled by the account of the following engagement, the British forces, under General Macdonald, comprising 1,000 men, also four guns and two maxims.

The whole history of war shows no parallel to the extraordinary action fought at Hot Springs, the tragical romance of it being heightened by the fact that it took place in the throne of the winds of the world, in a secret place of the earth under the shadow of the mighty snow-capped mountains. The Thibetan position extended for about a mile from the road under which the springs issue. Up the steep ridge the road was barred by a wall ending in a blockhouse. Walls were built on every fairly level spot on the ridge.

When Colonel Younghusband asked Brigadier-General Macdonald to get the Thibetans out of their position, if possible, without firing, our force was deployed and moved slowly up the ridge. The Thibetans manning the topmost wall, numbering about 200, surrendered without resistance, and allowed themselves to be disarmed. The remainder, however, obstinately held their places till our troops were within a few feet. They then sullenly retired towards the blockhouse, where the Lhassa general and other Thibetan officials were collected.

Within a short time, there was gathered between the blockhouse and the ridge a great mob of Thibetan soldiery. Estimates as to their number differ, but the place they occupied would have held a battalion in quarter column, and the Thibetans were shoulder to shoulder. The driving operation was carried out with the most admirable exactitude, the troops showing great self-restraint in not firing, although not knowing when the Thibetans might attack them.

When the Thibetans were all gathered together, Brigadier-General Macdonald, Colonel Younghusband, their staffs, the press correspondents, and others rode up to look at them. At this time the Thibetan rear was perfectly open, and they could have marched away if they had wished. The mob, nevertheless, stood together round the Lhassa general in a discontented frame of mind and muttering angry threats. Their attitude was sufficiently hostile to induce Brigadier-General Macdonald to order up two more companies of Pioneers with fixed bayonets. Presently there was a thin ring of Sikhs round the Thibetans, but no one dreamt of the terrible event which was impending.

The officers got off their horses; some sat down to eat sandwiches, and others brought out cameras. Suddenly a scuffle began in the north-eastern corner of the ring. The Thibetans shook their fists in the faces of the Sikhs and commenced throwing stones. The Lhassa general himself fired the first shot, blowing away a Sikh's jaw. A great tumult instantly arose. The Thibetans uttered a wild shout, drew their swords, and surged forward in all directions, firing their matchlocks. About a dozen swordsmen made a desperate rush in the direction of Brigadier-General Macdonald and the small knot of officers surrounding him.

Major Dunlop had two of his fingers slashed off. This assailant was shot down by Lieutenant Bignell. Four Thibetans made for Mr. Edmund Candler, *Daily Mail* correspondent, who was unarmed. He received no fewer than 12 wounds. Brigadier-General Macdonald himself shot down one of Mr. Candler's assailants at a few yards distance, and Lieutenant Davys, I.M.S., promptly killed two others, thus saving Mr. Candler from death. The other Thibetans, rushing forward, were met by revolver fire. Meanwhile, the Sikhs in front had drawn back a few yards, and met the Thibetans who were trying to climb over the wall with a terrible magazine fire. Four or five of the enemy actually climbed over the wall, and died like heroes.

One old man, armed with only a matchlock, sprang over the heaps of dead and deliberately kneeling down, well in advance of the others fired into the Sikhs. He was riddled with bullets. The Thibetans were so huddled together that they were unable either to use their swords or to fire. Many of them probably killed each other in their mad excitement. Finally, the mob surged to the rear, breaking through the ring of Sikhs.

The scenes that then followed were impressive and more awful than a fight in the cock-pit. The Thibetans, though their retreat was still open, disdained to scatter and run. They tramped away slowly and steadily, sullen and solemn, followed by a perfect hail of bullets. The mountain battery came into action and tore their line with shrapnel. A terrible trail of dead and dying marked their line of march. Finally, the last wounded Thibetan limped round the corner about 400 yards away. The grim tragedy was over. The whole affair did not last ten minutes, but in that short space of time the flower of the Thibetan Army perished.

The Thibetan general and the whole of his personal escort, as well as five high Lhassa officials were killed. Our own small losses are accounted for by the fact that the Thibetan swordsmen in the front rank could not reach the Sikhs, who had fixed bayonets, while the men in the middle of the mob were unable to use any weapon, but they all died game.

All those who witnessed the scene will carry for ever the memory of the grim, determined faces lighted with devildom and savagery. The Lhassa general himself undoubtedly provoked the fight, for in his interview with Colonel Younghusband his attitude was that of a man determined to either die or turn the Mission back. Part of the fearlessness shown by the Thibetans was undoubtedly due to want of knowledge of the effect of modern firearms, as well as contempt for the smallness of our forces.

The Thibetan soldiers outnumbered the wing of the Sikhs by six or seven to one. The impassive stolidity of the Sikhs of the 23rd and 32nd Pioneers deserves a word of admiration. Had they given way before the rush of the swordsmen, or had Brigadier-General Macdonald and the small knot of officers shown less personal courage, a disaster one does not care to dwell upon might have taken place. Colonel Younghusband and his staff were amongst the onlookers near the Thibetan soldiers, and were wholly unarmed.

The total British casualties were 12, but, besides these, two or three officers and a number of men received bruises from the flat edge of the

Thibetan swords. Immediately after our wounded had been attend-ed to, several officers with attendants went out among the wounded Thibetans scattered over the battlefield, binding up injured limbs, ad-ministering water, and applying field dressings to the wounded. Our troops provided dressing splints, hastily improvised from the muskets and scabbards abandoned by the enemy.

The Thibetan prisoners were employed in placing the wounded under shelter. The next day men were sent out from Turin, and a large number of wounded were brought into a house in the village, where Captain Baird and Lieutenant Day attended to them. They were evi-dently most grateful for these attentions. Some of them were to be seen cheerfully smoking cigarettes, and there were no signs of cring-ing in their manner, which rather suggested a proud and independent spirit.

www.ingramcontent.com/pod-product-compliance
Lightning Source LLC
Chambersburg PA
CBHW021055090426
42738CB00006B/350